D1072538

The
American Cowboy
THE MYTH & THE REALITY

WITHDRAWN

The American Cowboy

THE MYTH & THE REALITY

Joe B. Frantz *and*
Julian Ernest Choate, Jr.

 *Norman*

UNIVERSITY OF OKLAHOMA PRESS

Library of Congress Catalog Number 55-9629

Copyright 1955 by the University of Oklahoma Press,
Publishing Division of the University. Manufactured
in the United States of America. First edition,
October, 1955; second printing, by offset,
November, 1962.

To Our Parents
J. Ernest Choate AND *Emily Margaret Creed Choate*
AND
Ezra Allen Frantz AND *Mary Lavanna Buckley Frantz*

Preface

$\mathbf{A}$ couple or three years ago J. Frank Dobie wrote a book review expressing the sentiment, if not in the exact tangy wording, "Good Lord! Another book about the cowboy! What on earth for!" Since then, despite Mr. Dobie's mild choler, books about the cowboy continue to appear, and while we agree with the sage of the sagebrush that an evening with Horace or Socrates would be more profitable than ten nights with a book about cowboys, here we are adding to the bibliography of cowboy lore. The next time we meet Mr. Dobie we shall just have to look over his head.

The following study, however, has been pursued in something more than a spirit of perversity. The American cowboy has been examined every which way, natural and contrived, but he has hardly been looked at solemnly and reflectively in relation to his role in frontier history or as he appears in literature. Aspects of the cowboy have been presented in great and good detail, but we have sought here to issue a sort of short handbook which will depict the cowboy as a part of the whole Western panorama, instead of looking at him, as most previous works have done, in isolation from his larger environment.

Not that there haven't been some notable works on the cowboy. Everything that J. Evetts Haley has attempted has come off beautifully, but Haley, who could essay this re-evaluation much better than we, hasn't attempted a total assessment. For a short analysis, it is hardly likely that a better account of the cowboy will ever be written than the chapter that Paul Horgan brought out in 1954 in the second volume of his *Great River*. On reading it, our first reaction was to put on our typewriter cover and go home. But Horgan confines himself to a score of pages, which, however belletristic they may be, portray only the "feel" of the cowboy while leaving no room for the facts of him. Wayne Gard has said all that need ever be said about the Chisholm Trail, and Dobie has done the same for the longhorns and the mustangs. Their books are definitive, but again on phases of the cowboy portrait, not on the total picture. We could go on in this mood at some length.

The second part of our book concerns itself with critical interpretations of the earlier literature of the cowboy and with his later critics, which mark, we think, a real contribution. Thirty years ago E. Douglas Branch thrusted in this direction in his *The Cowboy and His Interpreters*, but Branch was working under a close time schedule, and his performance fell more than a little short. It is also thirty years old. Others have investigated the fiction of the cowboy, but invariably they did so in passing, as part of some other inquiry. The cowboy has carved a definite niche—niche nothing, it's a great gorge!—in American affection as a folk hero of substance and endurance, and in this role, too, we have surveyed him. But there is no need in giving away the story that lies in the pages ahead.

No man ever accomplishes anything entirely alone. Therefore we are grateful to such people as Miss Clara Brown, reference librarian for the Joint University Libraries, Vanderbilt University, and to Dr. Llerena Friend, librarian of the Eugene C. Barker Texas History Center of the University of Texas, for bibliographical aid; to Professors Henry Lee Swint, Donald Davidson, and Richmond Croom Beatty, all of Vanderbilt, and to Mr. J. Frank Dobie, of Austin, Professor Walter Prescott Webb of the University of Texas, and Mr. Fred R. Cotten, of Weatherford, Texas, for critical reading and perceptive suggestions; to Mrs. Kay Kendrick, University of Texas, for secretarial assistance; to Mr. Tom Brewer, University of Texas, for unflagging and imaginative work; to Miss Genevieve Boswell, Austin, for proofreading and indexing aid; to the Research Institute of the University of Texas, for financial aid; to Professor William R. Braisted of the University of Texas, Mrs. Ona Lee McKeen of the Library of Congress, and to Mr. Frank H. Wardlaw, director of the University of Texas Press, for help in obtaining illustrations and meeting deadlines; to Mrs. Mary Alice White Pettis of Washington, D. C., for permission to use the photographs of her brother, Erwin E. Smith; and to Marie Jones Choate and Helen Frantz, our wives, for making room for this effort in already crowded schedules.

J. B. F. AND J. E. C., JR.

Austin and Nashville
August 15, 1955

Preface ix

Table of Contents

List of Illustrations

The
American Cowboy
THE MYTH & THE REALITY

1. The Setting

A T MID-CENTURY William Boyd, a silver-haired movie actor three decades removed from romantic roles, can walk into almost any public gathering anywhere in the United States and promptly be mobbed by fans whose parents weren't even born when he began his long career before a Hollywood camera. Annually he grosses a million dollars on investments centered around a very minor literary creation named Hopalong Cassidy, written by a second-rate practitioner who learned cowboy lore and lingo hundreds of miles east of the Mississippi.

By 1952, Boyd's camera creation was being pictured on 63 television stations, heard over 152 radio stations, and read avidly in the comic strips of 155 newspapers. Boyd, or Cassidy, for the two have become synonymous (with, as one wag put it, Cassidy being the more synonymous of the two), was never any serious contender for acting awards, and his personal life, as viewed by the West Coast's professional gossips, has attained at least an average rating for matrimonial rowdiness. But nonetheless he is held up to the youth of America as a paragon, a person real and omnipresent, a man who can persuade Junior to hang up his clothes when parents can't, or to eat his body-building cereal with gusto when he finds it as insipid as would his parents—or Hopalong. What is Boyd's hold on American imagination? No matter how much critics may gibe at it, there is no denying the presence of such a hold. To young people, Cassidy is real; and to their more knowledgeable parents, he isn't much less real, for all they remind themselves "it's only a story."

And it's not just Boyd. The Lone Ranger "heigh-ho's" to his steady steed Silver over 250 radio and television stations, and on another 250 comic pages; Red Ryder upholds decency in 350 newspapers; and Roy Rogers in 175. Gene Autry, the original "Public Cowboy No. 1," has parlayed his homespun smile and what one critic called a "somnolent tenor" into a personal business empire whose worth in 1948 was variously estimated at between four and seven million dollars and still growing, and which includes such properties as these: his own movie company, a two million dollar rodeo, two music-publishing houses, a chain of four movie houses in the Dallas vicinity, three radio stations, two Phoenix, Arizona, newspapers, a California flying school, four big ranches in Texas, California, and Arizona, a major interest in a publishing company which turns out more than one million Gene Autry comic books a year, and royalties from nearly forty products (jeans, hair oil, cap pistols, hats, and so on) which net about 100,000 dollars a year. Again the question arises: How come?

A few more statistics to belabor the point. In 1951, civic organizations in 500 towns over the United States staged approved rodeos offering 1,750,000 dollars in prizes to watch some bow-legged strangers slither off their horses onto a steer's horns; 480 of the 2,400 movies issued by Hollywood were Westerns; one-fifth of the phonograph records sold were classified as Western and folk types; "Ghost Riders in the Sky," though often as not floating through a nightclub's cigarette and Old-Fashioned miasma, sung by some tuxedoed singer whose only acquaintance with a waterhole was the nearest bar, still sold two million copies; every movie star, male and female, who saw his popularity rating slipping quickly accepted a cowboy role in an effort to recapture his wandering public; and women in slacks cavorted across the open ranges of an estimated five hundred dude ranches.

In the world of the written word, Bantam Books issued twenty-five million Western titles between 1947 and 1951. The number of Western fiction titles listed in the *Book Review Digest* is creeping toward the one thousand mark, while fifty-four million people are estimated to have read Zane Grey. A *Saturday Evening Post* fiction editor told the authors that one reason his magazine ran so many cowboy stories was because the Western manuscripts submitted outnumbered all other types by three to one.

This is no latter-day situation. To reach back nearly a quarter of a century, Walter Prescott Webb, struck by the numerical domination of newsstands by Western-cowboy magazines, queried a group of Western publishers and found that their periodical sales ran usually somewhere between 250,000 and 1,500,000. And to go on back still another quarter-century, Owen Wister, that staunch friend of Theodore Roosevelt who in a sense started this continuing phenomenon of a cowboy-conscious America, saw his

The Virginian run through fifteen reprints in its first year.[1] And a little later, John A. Lomax, armed only with a claw-hammer coat, a hand b'iled shirt, and a collection of cowboy songs, caught the ear of the Eastern seaboard, fair Harvard included, and hasn't lost it yet.

Why this everlasting preoccupation with the cowboy in a country that is supposed to be crassly treadmilling its way to an ever increasing urbanization and ulcerated pursuit of happiness through money? Is it sectional—if so, why is the West the section? Is it occupational—if so, why the cowboy and not the logger, or the whaler, or the farmer, or the engineer who conquers mountains and tames rivers? Is it, as Walter Prescott Webb suggests, the romantic appeal of the Far Country—if so, why not, for instance, Alaska, which came into American consciousness at almost precisely the same time that the first cattle trailed their dusty way into Abilene?

The questions could go on and on, but "any fool can ask questions." And so, not wishing to appear any more foolish than comes natural, the authors would like to examine this cowboy myth and offer some answers, to try an evaluative and interpretative approach, to attempt to separate cowboy fact from fancy. With high seriousness and yet with the most genial intentions, we shall attempt to dissect the cowboy, realizing, of course, that he is apparently an eternal character who will not be fenced in, but will, instead, continue to go tearing across the open range, his horse's hoofs kicking up a dust-fog of legend that no amount of deadening analysis can ever settle.

[1] Marshall W. Fishwick, "The Cowboy: America's Contribution to the World's Mythology," *Western Folklore*, Vol. XI, No. 2 (April, 1952), 89. *Newsweek*, Vol. XXXVII (June 18, 1951), 56–57. *Life*, Vol. XXIV (June 28, 1948), 80–90. Burton Rascoe, "Opie Read and Zane Grey," *Saturday Review of Literature*, Vol. XXI, No. 3 (November 11, 1939), 8. Walter Prescott Webb, *The Great Plains*, 466, 480–482.

One thing, then, is clear at the outset. Sixty-five years after those small-souled homesteaders with their penchant for legality fenced in the tanks and put the plow to God's grasslands, killing off the range cattle industry, there still rides in our imaginative world just as many cowboys, just as many responsive horses, and just as many longhorns, mighty leathery though some of them may be by now. In many a Boot Hill may lie many a "Little Joe the Wrangler," but the Old West which they helped create lives just as vividly as it did when they were nervous and vital men swearing and swimming across the temperamental Canadian River and hoping to reach the crude delights of Kansas before they dried out entirely. The West lives on, and this book intends to do nothing to kill it off, no matter how inaccurately remembered and portrayed it may turn out to be.

In studying this lasting American folk hero, it will be impossible to avoid discursions, for the cowboy has appeared under such a variety of guises that he is inextricably entangled in the whole Western complex. Not only the cattleman's frontier but the other contemporary frontier enterprises must be considered, because as a legitimate folk hero the cowboy was not to be limited by space, distance, or occupation.

Thus we pick up the cowboy's trail in areas well removed from simple cow tending. He should be trailing— or driving, to use the more popular, if less exact, term— cattle northward on the Chisholm or Shawnee trails. But he is just as likely to be fighting a life-and-death stand with the Comanches or Apaches, or chasing the buffalo, or hunting a lost mine, or escorting an immigrant train 'way up along the Oregon Trail, or "bullwhacking" a load of freight to some remote ranch headquarters, or firing a transcontinental train, or saving the payroll as a range detective. And, of course, he is fanning his six-gun in a saloon brawl or riding pell-mell through the mesquite (a flesh-tearing feat which has deterred neither writers nor cameramen) in panting pursuit of a gang of cattle rustlers. Sheer fiction? Don't be hasty.

Actually the American cowboy is the composite, the blood-and-sinew prototype of all the frontiersmen who inhabited the region of the Great Plains in the latter half of the nineteenth century. In him are all the qualities and characteristics of every frontier folk hero from the Indian fighter of Daniel Boone's day forward. Yet ol' Dan Boone, though occupying a niche in American affections, never attained the following of the cowboy. The best literary exponent of Indian fighters east of the Mississippi is conceded to be James Fenimore Cooper, but a check at the circulation desk of any public library will quickly convince the curious that Cooper's fighters fail to fire the imagination of today's readers. The buffalo hunter, the mountain man, the gold washer, the Western immigrant, and the "bullwhacker" have come in for their share of interest, but not one of them carries much weight as a folk hero. Only the cowboy has captured and held the imagination of the American people with an interest undiminished by time.

A full-length documented study portraying the American cowboy as the American folk hero has yet to be made. Only cursory literary criticisms have appeared, either in journals or in chapters of books treating broader subjects. There is a reason for this situation. In the seventies and eighties the cowboy achieved a reputation, largely unsavory, which he has never quite lived down. The yellow press, the Beadle and Adams novels, Charles A. Siringo's highly bedecked autobiography, and Theodore Roosevelt's colorful championing all combined to present a highly distorted picture. Serious writers, therefore, have avoided the cowboy for fear they might wind up defending Zane Grey or Deadwood Dick of New York nickel-and-dime novel fame.

This reputation was confirmed and continued by Alfred Henry Lewis, Emerson Hough, Henry Wallace Phillips, Wister, Grey, and other writers early in the present century, in a pattern hardly changed today. Western writers are about as conservative a class as ever worked the literary field. They hit on a formula three-quarters of a century ago and, with few exceptions, have not dared depart from that formula since. The technique may have been honed to a finer edge, but the formula remains basic and unchanging. The result has been a portrait incomplete on the whole and untrue in many particulars, yet with a sufficient layer of truth to build a seemingly imperishable legend.

The truth is, as Bernard DeVoto pointed out in the 1930's, "thirty years of cheap fiction of the cattle kingdom about cowboys, rustlers, evil sheriffs, roundups, stampedes, six-guns, and branding irons have created an inertia which serious literature finds it hard to overcome." [2] But the fact that the West has been victimized by so many tawdry writers should not blind us to that literature of the West which is good nor to the fact that the Western does attract the occasional good writer, such as O. Henry, Hamlin Garland, or Eugene Manlove Rhodes. At this juncture, the heroic age in America is indisputably the age of the frontier, and there is no denying that the cowboy's segment of the frontier contains as much colorful and significant material about man versus man, man versus Nature, man versus environment, man versus emotion, man

[2] Bernard DeVoto, "Horizon Land (2)," *Saturday Review of Literature*, Vol. XV, No. 26 (April 24, 1937), 8.

versus temptation, man lonely, man in harness, man in motion, man developing—the stuff of which literature is made—as any other facet of the frontier from Jamestown forward that can be suggested. Walter Prescott Webb discusses one aspect of this viewpoint:

It has been customary to consider the trip over the Oregon Trail an heroic act, and it was; but in one sense it registered a lack of sufficient heroism to lead the people to undertake to live in the vast country that they traversed. They were in reality seeking the familiar and shunning the necessity of working out new ways in the Plains. The heroism lay in getting to Oregon and not in living there. The deserts, the waterless drives, the sand storms, the treacherous quicksands of the rivers, the prairie fires, the hostile Indians, the stampeding buffalo found on the Plains—all were a part of that great obstacle.[3]

American history is primarily responsible for making the cowboy into the folk hero he has become, and it is only through a sober glance at the cowboy's conditioning at the hands of history that we can assay properly the literature dealing with the cowboy. If the first Western railroad had connected San Antonio, say, with St. Louis, and if the immigrants had first settled Kansas instead of continent-hopping to the Pacific slopes, the cowboy would likely have been no more than an interesting occupational type, such as the Virginia City miner or even the Mexican *vaquero*. But transportation didn't reach southwestward at the beginning, and most settlers with a Western glint in their eyes originally looked on the vast unpeopled plains as the Great American Desert, and therefore to be avoided.

Into this enormous region, larger than all of the lands east of the Mississippi, came riding the Texas cowboy,

[3] Webb, *The Great Plains*, 149.

mounted on his Spanish mustang, singing to his longhorn herd. The forbidding desert, which had withstood the Spaniards and which, with towering mountains, was threatening to withstand Anglo-American encroachments as well, turned out not to be so forbidding after all when the right type of man, the cowboy, came along to utilize every foot of plains and mountains that would feed a steer. Within twenty years after the cowboy moved onto the last unsettled portion of the United States, a continuous line of inhabitants stretched from the Atlantic to the Pacific, for the cowboy had shown that this West had riches to plumb, fabulous wealth to yield to the hardy and adventurous, the sort of "risk-with-profit" that has always appealed to Americans. How this came about is worth a look.

The cowboy story, as every television viewer of three years knows by instinct if not by research, begins in Texas, builds to its peak in Texas, and then diffuses throughout the entire West, until almost every trans-Mississippi state contributes its share of threads to the whole tapestry. Three and one-half centuries before the first Texan cantered into Abilene, Kansas, in 1867, the longhorn cattle industry was unloaded by the Spanish *Conquistadores* at Vera Cruz. Largely untended and unvalued, except for their hides, these cattle slowly worked their way toward the Rio Grande to the north, taking time to multiply as they came. By the time Texas had been divorced from Mexico long enough to consider itself capable of joining the other ten Southern states in secession, the range cattle industry in Texas was, from an Anglo-American viewpoint, three decades old, while from a Latin-American viewpoint its age was measured in generations. Twenty-five years after the Civil War, the range cattle industry occupied nearly an identical historical and sentimental position in such un-Texan areas as the Canadian border, Montana, Oregon, and Arizona, so it is no breach of geographical reality that the first Western novel to be accepted seriously, Wister's *Virginian*, lays its base in Wyoming and shows a disposition to move farther from Texas all the time.

The cowboy then, though a Texan in his first generation, soon came to be a citizen of the whole of the Western frontier, and in considering him, his role as a frontiersman should remain always in the background of our thinking. His frontier was a short-lived frontier, lasting only twenty-five years; but even if he hadn't become a romantic and romanticized figure, he would still have come in for some share of serious attention because of his participation in one portion of the frontier experience, a portion which Frederick Jackson Turner called the greatest pastoral movement in recorded history.

When in 1893 young Turner read his classic, "The Significance of the Frontier in American History," before the American Historical Association, he gave rise to a whole new school of frontier historians, as well as an academic and intellectual furor which hasn't subsided to this day. In his paper, Turner claimed that the "true point of view in the history of this nation is not the Atlantic coast, it is the Great West" so recently conquered by the Anglo-American. The validity of Turner's thesis is of no concern here, but the fact that he set men to work examining and re-evaluating American history and literature, with the consequence that still more frontier history and literature were spawned, is important. In the new interest in the frontier which Turner stirred, the cowboy was not forgotten.

Since any study of the cowboy must necessarily include his place as a frontiersman who conquered the

Great Plains, Turner's definition of the frontier is pertinent to this study. According to his definition, the frontier existed within the United States wherever Anglo-American forces were transforming a virgin wilderness into a civilized community. It was, he said, "the outer edge of the wave—the meeting point between savagery and civilization." [4] Across the Great American Desert, on the outer edge of this wave, at the meeting point between savagery and civilization, rode the cowboy, playing his crude but effective civilizing role. Eight years before Turner first nailed up his thesis on the door of history, Joseph Nimmo, Jr., author of one of the earliest and best accounts of the spread of the cattleman's frontier, recognized the cowboy's civilizing influence in the following words:

In the course of a few years, hundreds of thousands of cattle, almost all of them driven from the state of Texas as yearlings and two-year-olds, quietly grazing through the former haunts of the buffalo, and the cowboy, armed and equipped, a bold rider and valiant in fight, became the dominating power through the vast areas where a few years before the Indian had bidden defiance to the advancement of the arts of civilization. The question of Indian wars was thus forever settled in the region mentioned. [5]

Pathfinder and empire builder, the cowboy explored nearly every mile of the High Plains. Riding with only the sun and the stars for his compass and with only a setting sun or an empty belly as a timepiece, he moved through mountain passes of the highest ranges, across waterless plains and hostile Indian country, from the Rio Grande to the Canadian border, and from the Red River to the Yellowstone, until he crossed every divide and nosed his mustang into every draw from the eastern shadows of the

[4] Frederick Jackson Turner, "The Significance of the Frontier," *The Frontier in American History*, 1, 3.
[5] Joseph Nimmo, Jr., *Range and Ranch Cattle Traffic*, 10.

Rockies to the seaward side of the Sierra Nevada. In the process he shaped and forged that character which Turner ascribed to the American frontiersman when he said:

The result is that to the frontier the American intellect owes its striking characteristics. That coarseness and strength combined with acquisitiveness; that practical, inventive turn of mind, quick to find expedients; that masterful grasp of material things, lacking in the artistic but powerful to effect great ends; that restless nervous energy; that dominant individualism, working for good and evil, and withal that buoyancy and exuberance which comes with freedom—these are the traits of the frontier, or traits called out elsewhere because of the existence of the frontier.[6]

Whatever truth there may be in Turner's statement regarding the heritage handed on to Americans by their frontier predecessors, he described the cowboy as he is seen by these authors, and as he will be seen in the chapters ahead. A discrepancy exists between the range cowboy as he has been presented fictionally and as he actually was. A folk hero he has become, with no present evidence that his unique position is on the wane. If for every truth that is told about the cowboy each year in poem, novel, and ballad—and let us state right here that to us truth need not be strictly factual if it will just capture the essence—there is a matching untruth, exaggeration, or caricature; if for every good story that emerges concerning the cowboy there are concomitant inanities; and if the cowboy, operating on a vast canvas studded with dramatic possibilities, has largely been missed by the writers of great literature, are these things the fault of the cowboy or do they lie with the limited vision of those people who approach the cowboy's story? Let us see.

[6] Turner, "The Significance of the Frontier," *The Frontier in American History,* 37.

2. The Beginning

THE American cowboy exists on three distinct levels—the historical level, about which the average American cares and knows no more than he does about any other phase of nonmilitary or nonpolitical history; the fictional level, in which the cowboy occupies a not quite respectable but highly popular position; and the folklore level, on which the cowboy sits as an idealized creation of the American folk mind. In this chapter the emphasis will be on the historical level in order that a foundation may be laid for a later examination of the fictional cowboy and the cowboy folk hero.

When in 1865 the Civil War drew to a close, the Far West was largely unpopulated from the prairie regions west of the Mississippi across the High Plains to the Rockies. The later states of Idaho, Utah, Nevada, and Arizona held only a handful of Anglo-Americans. In Nevada, Montana, and Wyoming were mining camps, but they were almost wholly isolated from the outside world. At the western base of the Rocky Mountains, the Mormons were living a largely detached existence, shunned by other Americans and to a degree glad of it. Truthfully, the Great Plains still belonged to the Indian, be he a Comanche or Apache in the Southwest or a Sioux or Cheyenne in the North. In the tall shadows of the Rockies, a few mountain men still worked, as they had for half a century, setting their traps and caching their furs, but they were quiet, almost furtive men, and their numbers had sharply declined during the preceding twenty-five years. About the only commercial sound was the creaking of a freighting wagon belonging to Russell, Majors, and Waddell as it made its way overland.

Far to the south, almost in another world, lay the state of Texas, half frontier and half southern, with its frontier half swarming with four million longhorns waiting for a market. Texas alone was larger than the original thirteen states, and the Great Plains of which it was a part covered one and one-third million square miles; or 44 per cent of the total area of the United States, or an area equal to Great Britain, Ireland, France, Germany, Denmark, Holland, Belgium, Austria, Italy, Spain, Portugal, and one-fifth of European Russia. There was magnitude here— land magnitude, and the longhorn cattle age appropriated all of it.

As already noted, the Great Plains existed in the American imagination as the Great American Desert, a boundless, trackless, worthless area fit only for savage Indians and wild beasts, a land of cactus and prairie dogs, of shifting sands and tall eccentric whirlwinds of dust. As late as the Civil War, it was still fashionable, according to one 1905 account, to

. . . attribute to this almost unknown region every conceivable horrid aspect, and dreadful condition supposed to be inseparable from great deserts. Imaginative writers wrought these into weird tales, and picture makers were inspired to some most extraordinary performances . . . the desolate barren land of horrors that constituted the Great American Desert. . . . According to all these fantastic tales, the water-less, windswept land of sand and stone, this howling, hopeless, worthless cactus-bearing waste inhabited by savages of extreme fierceness and cruelty, and haunted by prowling beasts of unexampled ferocity, were joined to a mountain region in the far West where towering mountain peaks tore all the passing clouds to tatters, where snow that fell before Columbus landed still was under snow that had fallen since, where the naked granite sides of the mountains went straight aloft until lost to view, where shrieking gales forever blew over the frozen desolation that reigned supreme, and as they drove along, wailed out the warning to rash mankind: "abandon hope, ye who enter here." [1]

This myth of the Great American Desert existed in the American mind for the first half of the nineteenth century and continued to some extent right down till the next century was ready to pick it up. Environmental conditions, it was said, would make its investment by Anglo-Americans out of the question. As late as the 1870's, Jay Cooke, the country's foremost securities salesman at the time, failed in part to sell Northern Pacific bonds, bringing down about his head his banking empire and helping to precipitate a protracted panic, because his road had to traverse

[1] *Prose and Poetry of the Livestock Industry of the United States*, 343–344.

that presumably untenable region between Minnesota and the Pacific Coast. Any number of geographies, histories, and atlases published between 1820 and 1850 supported the myth with printed charts and descriptions.

The foundation for the misconception had been laid as early as 1541, when Coronado had written his king that the region was a desert. Among American explorers, Lewis and Clark and Zebulon Montgomery Pike did little to lay the myth, while in 1859 Horace Greeley, a man of audience if not exactly of letters, helped along the legend with an exaggerated account in his New York *Tribune*. There were other contributors, but it is not the purpose here to do more than point out a few.

What is important is that a Great American Desert did exist in the American imagination, and that the cowboy was affected by its existence. For one thing, the cowboy trailed his herds into that fearsome desert, exploding if not permanently dispersing the belief that reasonably civilized men and beasts could not live and prosper there. On the other hand, the feeling that the Old West, with its rock-ribbed mountains, its sheer canyons, and its waterless wastelands, was fabulously formidable became so deeply imbedded in American thinking that Western fiction produces an automatic state of mind and a sense of setting which conditions both writer and reader before the story ever gets underway.

A part of this Great American Desert lay in an area which most Texans would describe as "below" San Antonio, a trapezoidal area running westward to Laredo, down the Rio Grande to Brownsville, up along the Gulf Coast to Indianola (an important entrepot then, but a ghost town today), and then northward to San Antonio again. In this capacious region between the Nueces River and the Rio Grande was spawned the range cattle indus-

try as symbolized by the longhorn. It was
cattle country. The climate is mild, with
sional blue norther barreling in to remind one
parts of the world winter is made for shiverin
just enough brush—timber is too dignified a wo
scrub and mesquite that are all about—to offe.
tion to the cattle in inclement weather; and in the
there was usually sufficient water and grass, which i
than can be said in the 1950's. The country had the fu
advantage of being too close to San Antonio and o
lesser centers to attract more than just an occasional
dian raider. Cattle put out to graze could munch u
molested and could frolic biologically without fear o
decimating interruptions.

For generations, Mexicans had cradled cattle in this
Nueces country, unbothered by Anglo-American en-
croachment until in the 1820's, when the two Austins—
first Moses, the father, and then Stephen, his son—in an
effort to redress their lead mine losses in Missouri obtained permission to settle colonists in an area to the
northeast. Other *empresarios* received later grants, and individual American immigrants pursued their natural penchant for spilling over prescribed boundaries, so that by
the time the Texas revolution broke out in the fall of 1835
the eastern portion of the future state was rather well
blanketed with settlers. But the Nueces Valley remained
relatively untouched, a sort of no man's land, a Texas
desert. Nothing about the Republic of Texas, which lasted
for a somewhat delicate decade, did anything to disturb
this condition, and about the only attention the Nueces
country received from the Texans, aside from such corner
spots as Corpus Christi and Brownsville, was an occasional crisscross skirmish between Mexicans and Texans as
the Mexicans sought to place the Texas boundary along

The Beginning 19

the Nueces and the Texans with superior stubbornness insisted on the Rio Grande. Once the Texans had clinched the Rio Grande, they appropriated all of the Spanish stock which the Mexicans in their retreat southward had been unable to take across the river and promptly declared through their congress that all unbranded cattle were public property.[2]

Whence came these longhorns? Originally tended for a thousand years by the Moors on the plains of northern Africa and Andalucia, they had arrived in Santo Domingo as part of the cargo of Columbus' second voyage. In 1521, about the time that Cortes was consorting with the Malinche, Gregorio de Villalobos transported a load from the West Indian island to New Spain. Other shipments followed not too far behind, and the Spanish cattle had arrived on the North American mainland to stay. By 1540, they had so multiplied that when Coronado gathered together his considerable caravan to seek the golden cities of Cibola, he included five hundred head of cattle with no great effort. Thus were the first cattle of any description introduced within the present boundaries of the United States. Meanwhile bovine biological processes, uninhibited by any inimical restraints, worked with such steadiness that twenty-five years after Coronado passed through, Francisco de Ibarra could report that lower Sinaloa was teeming with cattle, while by the end of the century one Jalisco owner was reportedly branding thirty thousand calves a year.

The first cattle of consequence to arrive in Texas came a century and a half later, when the Spaniards trailed two hundred head from below the Rio Grande to the eastern Texas mission they were establishing eight miles west of

[2] Webb, *The Great Plains*, 210. According to Mexican law, unbranded stock was also state property.

the Neches River as a buffer against the French. Here, in the flavorsome words of J. Frank Dobie, "the seed were certainly sown for a stock to become in time more famous than the wild cattle of Chillingham and wilder and fiercer than those 'strong bulls of Bashan'." [3] By the time that the Anglo-Americans began to enter Texas in 1821, wild cattle roamed the entire area between the Rio Grande and the Red River. *Wild* here is a precise word, for they ran in small bunches, usually at night, keeping to the thickets. To the early colonists they were little more—or little less—than game animals. These were the first Texas longhorns.

To paraphrase the old college alumnus, they don't make cattle like the longhorns anymore. Certainly not in looks, and most certainly not in imagination. Horns, their most conspicuous feature, ran usually somewhere between three and five feet in length, frequently doubling up and backward half their distance. Tall, bony, coarse-headed and coarse-haired, flat-sided, thin-flanked, sway-backed, big-eared, with tails dragging the ground and legs that belonged to a race horse, they lumbered through the brasada and over the plain, grotesque to the critical eye and beautiful to the sentimentalist cowboy. Dobie, who didn't learn his descriptions from a book, has described them thus:

mightily antlered, wild-eyed, this herd of full-grown Texas steers might appear to a stranger seeing them for the first time as a parody of their kind. But however they appeared, with their steel hoofs, their long legs, their staglike muscles, their thick skins, their powerful horns, they could walk the roughest ground, cross the widest deserts, climb the highest mountains, swim the widest rivers, fight off the fiercest bands of wolves,

[3] "The First Cattle in Texas and the Southwest Progenitors of the Longhorns," *Southwestern Historical Quarterly*, Vol. XLII, No. 3 (January, 1939), 176.

endure hunger, cold, thirst, and punishment as few beasts of the earth have ever shown themselves capable of enduring.[4]

The longhorn is gone, confined to a government refuge or some banker's play-ranch, but no one who saw him, three thousand strong, picking his curiously fastidious way across miles of verdant prairie trailed by the hired man on horseback, will ever forget the thrill this side of immortality. Dobie responded to the call of the longhorn with the following words:

In picturesqueness and romantic realism his name is destined for remembrance as long as the memory of man travels back to those pristine times when waters ran clear, when free grass waved a carpet over the face of the earth, and America's man on horseback . . . rode over the rim with all the abandon, energy, insolence, pride, carelessness, and confidence epitomizing the becoming West.[5]

If first reaction to the sight of a longhorn provoked a feeling of disbelief, there was nothing to give pause in the visual aspect of the second member of the triad which emerged from the Nueces cradle. The Spanish mustang looked like a scrub of no particular parentage. But no animal ever belied appearances more, for he was the instrument on whom the cowboy depended for his very survival. Cowboys weren't meant to walk, and the High Plains weren't designed for walkers. There was only one thing a cowboy feared as much as a decent woman, observed E. C. Abbott—and that was being set afoot. A man on the plains without a horse was like a man overboard at sea, prey to anything the plains had to offer—distance

---

[4] *The Longhorns*, 41–42.
[5] *Ibid.*, xiii–xiv.

from waterholes, predatory Indians, or wild beasts, even wild cattle, or not-so-wild cattle. The longhorns were so accustomed to seeing cowboys on horseback that a man dismounted among them could easily be trampled in a stampede. But a man on horseback was a superior being who could rule elemental Nature and could triumph over an adverse environment. The affection between man and mount, cemented through months of sharing privation and danger and adventure, was therefore an almost human thing; and many a cowboy, as Paul Horgan points out, would gladly share the last of his water canteen with his horse rather than see his equine friend go thirsty.[6]

Like the longhorn, the mustang was of Spanish descent, with strong blood ties to the barb, originally brought into Spain by the Moors from North Africa. When Columbus was weighing anchor at Cadiz for his second voyage of discovery, the mustang was put aboard. Once in the New World, he underwent radical changes to meet a merciless environment that demanded unequaled endurance and stamina. The horse that emerged was not much larger than a stocky pony, but he had the strength, coupled with the intelligence, to outwork any half-dozen Eastern horses. Most important of all, he had "cow sense." Instinctively he knew how to control longhorns, as sensitive as a suitor to their changing moods. If

[6] Paul Horgan, *Great River: The Rio Grande in North American History*, 879. M. H. Donoho, *Circle-Dot*, 149. Andy Adams, *The Log of a Cowboy*, 382. Perhaps the tenderest tribute ever paid the mustang came from the pen of the unsentimental Cortes, who wrote his cavalier-emperor of a mare which had galloped toward the enemy, only to be wounded. Wrote Cortes, as though of a *compadre:* "She, when she saw their wickedness, though badly wounded, came back to us. That night she died and though we felt her death, . . . our grief was less, as she did not die in the power of the enemy." And to show further the acceptance of the horse as a comrade, there is this passage from Bernal Díaz: "Now I will set down the names of all the horses and mares that accompanied us to this conquest." R. B. Cunninghame Graham, *The Horses of the Conquest*, 25.

necessary, he could snap like a feist dog at the rump of a straying steer.[7]

By the time the Anglo-Americans arrived in the West, the Indians had already learned the value of the mustang, and with his aid, they prolonged their control of some portions of the plains almost until the close of the nineteenth century. Especially they used him for hit-and-run forays on outlying ranches, scattering horses and cattle as they pillaged and burned. On arrival in Texas and the West, the Americans discovered that the mustang had unexcelled qualities as a cow horse, frequently being more skilled than his rider at doing the right thing at the right time. On a dark night, with a norther yowling in all its mournful Arctic fury, with the cattle stampeding over rough and unfamiliar ground, and with the uncertain cowboy wondering which way was which, the manner in which a mustang carried his master, never stumbling or falling, hardly faltering, seemed little short of marvelous to the plains cowboy. The mustang was, in the words of one of his historians, a "natural-born cow-horse," and without him and his companion longhorn "part of America could never have been built."[8] Given a southerner with inbred equestrianism, a saddle a man could stick to, a lariat, and a double-cinched mustang who knew as much about a longhorn as his rider, and you had the tools for an industry, the tools to work and mold the resource, the Texas longhorn.

Actually the antecedents of the cattle culture of the Great Plains reach far back into the days of Colonial history. Spanish methods of handling cattle on horseback had entered the colonies by way of Louisiana, when Spanish influences dominated the social and cultural patterns

[7] Robert Moorman Denhardt, *The Horse of the Americas*, 29–30, 175–78. Dobie, *The Mustangs*, 305–14.
[8] Denhardt, *The Horse of the Americas*, 175–76.

of that region. But Anglo-Americans, too, made their contributions. Long before they became concerned about the desert barrier to the west, Americans were grazing cattle on the public lands of Virginia and the Carolinas, periodically rounding up cattle that had been ranging over miles of frontier territory and behaving like Beëlzebub when the roundup was completed. Stationed across the Atlantic Piedmont were occasional "cowpens" into which cattle, bearing brands to identify ownership, were herded by "cattle hunters," the ante-bellum equivalents of Western cowboys, and every bit as ornery. Three or four men could handle a herd of up to five hundred.[9] A British official, writing in the late Colonial period, paints a picture of the cattle industry in South Carolina and Georgia that, with the substitution of an occasional word or place name, could easily be a picture of the later West. Great herds he saw, moving "under the auspices of cowpen keepers . . . from forest to forest as the grass wears out or the planters approach them." [10]

When the Eastern cowman moved west, he took his lore and his vocabulary with him, so that the line of derivation is distinct, with here and there a modification in method or a change in terminology, as in the substitution of the more colorful "roundup" for "cowhunt" and the Spanish "corral" for "cowpen." Owen Wister's *Virginian* then need not have been a raw Yankee come to Wyoming, but could have been a man whose ancestors chased cattle rustlers—or *thieves* in Virginia—into the Shenandoah uplands. President Theodore Roosevelt, every bit as proud of

[9] Robert L. Meriwether, *The Expansion of South Carolina, 1729–1765*, 12. Philip Alexander Bruce, *Economic History of Virginia in the Seventeenth Century*, I, 477. William Darby, *The Immigrant's Guide*, 76–77.
[10] Frank L. Owsley, "The Pattern of Migration and Settlement on the Southern Frontier," *Journal of Southern History*, Vol. XI, No. 2 (May, 1945), 151.

his cowboying as of his political successes, saw the pattern emerge in this manner:

The rough rider of the plains, the hero of the rope and revolver, is first cousin to the backwoodsman of the southern Alleghenies, the man of the ax and rifle; he is only a unique offshoot of the frontier stock of the Southwest. The very term "round-up" is used by the cowboys in the exact sense in which it is employed by the hill people and mountaineers of Kentucky, Tennessee, and North Carolina.[11]

Here then were some basic ingredients for the making of a unique industry, when after the Civil War the Texans, war losers but not poor losers, came home to pick up and remake the pieces of their lives shattered by rebellion. There was the myth of the Great American Desert, a physical force to be reckoned with; there was the industry's animate trinity—the American cowboy, his Texas longhorn, and his Spanish mustang; and there was a stock lore of Colonial origins carried westward to Texas on the tide of immigration. In a state hardly touched by an invader, property in Texas was still intact but untended, and the people were impoverished and interrupted, but not permanently impaired. Texans were, in the words of Emerson Hough, poverty stricken "amid such bounty of wild Nature as no other part of this great republic has ever known," a statement which, though a bit exaggerated, contains more than a germ of truth.[12] How then to get back on a profitable path?

One way—in retrospect, an obvious way—was through the cattle industry. While men had been making war a thousand miles away, cattle had been cared for by those

[11] *Ranch Life and the Hunting Trail*, 22. See also Joseph Schafer, *The Social History of American Agriculture*, 97.
[12] *North of 36*, p. 9.

who were left—old men, children, and Negro slaves. "Cared for" is all that was done, however, and virtually no attempt at cattle marketing had been pursued except on a local basis. Lack of transportation took care of that.

Now there were cattle, literally millions of cattle— estimates run between three and one-half and four and three-fourths millions—in the Nueces Valley, worth three to four dollars a head in Texas, if you could find a buyer with that kind of money, or worth thirty to forty dollars a head in Kansas City and St. Louis, if you could find transportation. But again, transportation in Texas was almost nonexistent, and no present relief was in sight. The problem was that of bringing a resource to its market. The pot of gold was there, in sight, but how does one get to the end of the rainbow?

For a generation Texans had gained experience in chasing a cattleman's rainbow, trailing longhorns into Missouri to supply California immigrant trains with work stock and to sell beef to the inhabitants of those communities to which they took their herds. St. Louis, Chicago, and even New York received herds in 1854, the New York herd having laid over for the winter in Illinois, walked on to Muncie, Indiana, and entrained there for Manhattan, where they were observed with both idle and commercial curiosity, bringing up to eighty dollars a head.[13] But the trail to the north and east was not a trail of happiness, either bovine, human, or economic. For the longhorn carried a tick which left less hardy cattle with which he came

[13] Wayne Gard, "The Shawnee Trail," *Southwestern Historical Quarterly,* Vol. LVI, No. 3 (January, 1953), 359, 364–67. *Life of Tom Candy Ponting,* 27–42. The Longhorns didn't impress favorably all New Yorkers. Wrote a former president of the state agricultural society a decade and a half later: "We should hardly speak of this strange race of animals, were it not that of late years they have found their way . . . into our seaboard markets." Lewis F. Allen, *American Cattle: Their History, Breeding, and Management,* 174.

in contact ill with Spanish—or as it soon became known, Texas—fever, a form of bovine typhoid which could annihilate whole herds, as the owners of the dead and dying cattle in western and central Missouri could testify with some natural heat. By the beginning of the Civil War, Texas trail drivers were not welcome in Missouri because their cattle weren't welcome.

Another drive possibility lay to the Gulf coast, where the cattle could be shipped to New Orleans, a route that had been tried since the 1840's. One Beaumont, Texas, diarist reported that in one year an estimated forty thousand had crossed the Neches headed eastward. The way west was another route, as the forty-niners had demonstrated when they drove cattle to the gold fields of California well in advance of most Texan trailers. As San Francisco boomed and the little city of the angels to the southward struggled in the 1850's, cattle were pointed from Texas in increasing thousands, as a steer which could be purchased for upwards of five dollars in Texas might bring as high as one hundred and sixty dollars on the coast.[14] But it hadn't been easy money, for the California trail carried dangers that dwarfed those encountered later along the more renowned Chisholm Trail, and the California route became a graveyard for footsore, abandoned cattle; for cattle with throats aflame, with only dust and sun to slake them for too many miles on end; for cattle poisoned on alkali water; for horses whose hoofs were cut to the quick by the *malpais* ridges; and even for cowboys who met more Apache and white brigands than they could handle.[15] Prices were high, true; but the distance was long, and the toll on man and beast frequently disastrous.

[14] Joseph G. McCoy, *Historic Sketches of the Cattle Trade of the West and Southwest*, 23–26. Robert Glass Cleland, *The Cattle on a Thousand Hills*, 102–110.

[15] James G. Bell, "A Log of the Texas–California Cattle Trail," *Southwestern Historical Quarterly*, Vol. XXXV, No. 3 (January, 1932), 208 ff.

It was a case of simply following a generation of precedent when in 1866 the Texas cattlemen looked at their herds, thought of the market hundreds of miles away, and determined to walk with their cattle to that market and its pot of gold. The result was that more than a quarter of a million longhorns crossed the Red River heading north out of Texas in that first full year after the war. The drives moved along with deceptive smoothness until the herds hit the Missouri-Kansas pocket around Baxter Springs, where they were first met by groups of insolent armed mobs who stole, stampeded, or stopped the cattle on a pretext of halting the advance of Texas fever. Resist the ruffians and death might result, or a portion of the area might become a litter of cattle killed in wild plunges off Ozark cliffs, of cattle with broken legs and broken horns, and of cattle that ran off into the darkness never to be seen by their owner again, unless he chose to pay the mob several dollars a head to round up the cattle they had driven off with a wildly flapping buffalo blanket in the first place. Could the prairies talk, wrote Joseph McCoy, "they could tell many a thrilling, blood-curdling story of carnage, wrong, outrage, robbery and revenge not excelled in the history of any banditti or the annals of the most bloody savages." [16]

If somehow the Texans pushed their herds past the ruffians in a reasonably intact state, their difficulties were likely to continue, for irate farmers, remembering the devastations of Texas fever after previous longhorn visits, would demand a halt until cold weather could set in to nullify the fever-bearing tick. If the Texan, his eyes on the market, determined to continue, he might find himself beaten or even killed, just as likely by some deadly serious farmer protecting his herd as by a border bully bent only on bedevilment. Or if the Texan weren't harmed, he might

[16] *Historic Sketches,* 96.

see his cattle shot down, which was nearly as bad to a cowboy who had worried with the longhorns over hundreds of miles of weary trailing. More discreet Texans turned their herds back into the Indian country to await winter, only to find that prairie fires had destroyed much of the grass and that the cattle must either be driven farther or deserted. The result of the whole attempt was that in 1866 only a comparative handful of the 260,000 cattle which had left Texas ever reached a market.[17] The pot of gold still beckoned, but because of human obstacles it was as elusive as ever.

As 1867 approached, Texas cattlemen must have asked themselves and each other, "What to do?" What they couldn't know was that at the far end of the trail another man was asking himself the same question and finding an answer. A tall, loud-talking, visionary Illinoisan named Joseph G. McCoy, not quite thirty years old, had been fattening and forwarding livestock for a half-dozen years. As a middleman seeking his commission, he needed an ample supply of his particular commodity, and the largest supply lay in Texas, or halfway between, halted by farmers or bandits. McCoy thought he perceived a solution to the problem, his problem, and in the best American tradition helped to give birth to another tradition, the Western cowboy whose striking characteristics were associated with the six-shooter, lariat, chaps, sombrero, chuck wagon, roundup, and branding iron, not to mention wind and drought and danger.

McCoy was looking for a site along a Western railroad that cattle could be driven to, traded, and loaded for shipment eastward. He had tried the Missouri Pacific in St. Louis and, in one of the historic bad commercial guesses of all time, had been all but thrown out of the president's

[17] Edward Everett Dale, *The Range Cattle Industry*, 50, 53.

office, with the result that he had next sought the services of a lesser line, the Hannibal and St. Joseph, which had agreed to co-operate with McCoy and the Kansas Pacific in seeing that cattle were taken into Chicago with reasonable facility and at a profitable rate. Thus Chicago became the world's butcher, and thus St. Louis became a major city but no international meat market.

With his transportation arrangements perfected, McCoy established in Abilene, Kansas, a "small, dead place . . . of about one dozen log huts," but well watered and grassy.[18] Beginning in July, 1867, he went into a sixty-day building program to get ready to "make" a cattle town where only two small business houses and the inevitable saloon now existed, to make the first of the turbulent, booming, lawless Kansas cowtowns that have so enriched the American picture. Shortly, a shipping yard was set up, a large pair of Fairbanks scales installed, a cattle barn and an office completed, and a hotel partially completed. Railway loading and switching facilities were prepared. Everything was ready—everything, that is, except cattle.

To obtain cattle, McCoy sent an Illinois associate, W. W. Sugg, on a two hundred-mile ride into the Indian country to locate any drovers who might be undecided about their destination and to divert them to Abilene. Although Abilene lay within the area forbidden to longhorns by Kansas law, Sugg assured the doubtful drovers that the trail to Abilene lay far enough west of settlement that their cattle would not be molested. Somewhat reluctantly, some drovers were persuaded and pointed their lead steers for the new cattle depot.

By early August, seven thousand cattle had reached Abilene, and before the end of the season twenty-five thousand would arrive. On September 5, the first ship-

[18] McCoy, *Historic Sketches*, 116–17.

ment, twenty carloads, rattled off for Chicago, and Abilene was dousing itself in good cheer.[19] When McCoy felt he was on the threshold of an era, no truer prophet ever lived. For the next half-dozen years, Abilene was to become a town the like of which had never been seen before. Abilene, more than four hundred miles north of the Red River and nearly a thousand miles from the Nueces country, was to become the commercial capital of Texas as the next year the number of bovine arrivals doubled, only to more than redouble the year after that. A town which in later years was to be the home of a future president, but which as recently as the spring of 1867 found its one saloon keeper piecing out his income by selling prairie dogs at five dollars a head to railroad tourists, Abilene was to know a prosperity, a lustiness, and a greed which would make it legend wherever cattlemen stopped to talk. It would be superseded by other and better towns, but whenever stories of the range cattle industry and of cowboys appeared, Abilene would be the first and most fondly remembered, for Abilene was in at the beginning. In Abilene, the Texas cowboy was discovered and first became a distinct type, and here he first displayed for a national audience those extremes of temperament that make a hero.

[19] Gard, *The Chisholm Trail*, 55, 65–69.

3. The Trail

In the story of the American frontiers, the cattle trail provides the fragments of poetry along the narrative way. And particularly the Chisholm Trail, which, strung across a thousand miles of prairie, has enriched American folk music in the dozens of ballads composed about it. Actually, the Chisholm Trail exists as a myth in the American imagination. And though few people might know its location, and not many more have an understanding of the problems facing the early trail driver on his way through a wilderness, yet it is a safe assertion that the Texas cowboy would never have become an American folk hero if it had not been for the Chisholm and Western trails—trails leading out of and through virgin lands long thought habitable only by wild Indians.

Aside from the ballad folk artists and, of course, the ubiquitous research historians, writers of Western literature have had little worthwhile to say about the cattle trails, not even about the Chisholm Trail. Only two novels of any merit have been written about the Chisholm Trail, Emerson Hough's *North of 36* and Andy Adams' *Log of a Cowboy* (which goes beyond the Chisholm limits), despite the series of bold adventures along its way that are almost unique in the American frontier experience. Here the trail drivers gained their honor and distinction as intrepid pioneers, and here, too, they achieved—and sometimes it was truly an achievement—their bad reputations when the worst of them literally "shot up" the frontier towns at the end of their long ride northward.

A closer look at trail driving then is in order, for though the trail may not have supplied "literature," which can be a pompous word at times, the trail did furnish the basic materials for generations of American cowboy myths and stories. The cowboy went incidentally about being frontiersman and pathfinder for an empire while fundamentally, he thought, trying to bring resource and market together. He trailed for a maximum of thirty years, and most of his trailing was done between 1870 and 1885—a short generation only—but in that time he and forty thousand other cowboys headed out somewhere with their herds. These were bold men, courageous men, aware that danger was real and that over the next swell of prairie might wait the untamed Comanche or that a sudden sound might send the herd stampeding, death in every hoof, so that not every companion who rode away that morning was guaranteed safe passage till the next morning.

There is no avoiding the fact that the primary symbol of the mythology which has grown around the cattle kingdom has a distinctly Texas cast, no matter how weary

Erwin E. Smith: Library of Congress

BIG COUNTRY AND NO SHELTER. Here a cow hand
shields a small fire with his slicker in the rain.

Erwin E. Smith: Library of Congress

Two Down, More Comin'. Branding calves on the open range required co-ordination, tough-fibered men, and long hours.

much of the nation has grown of the professionally gar-
rulous Texan. At the moment, no other collection of men
was fitted to grapple with the Great American Desert and
its hostile forces, and it can be argued with some effectiveness whether any other group of Americans could have
been found who would have been willing, as well fitted
or not, to accept the challenges of nature and distance and
danger. True, cowboys showed up all over the plains
areas, but it was the Texas cowboy who taught his northern cousin the techniques of handling cattle in the vast-
nesses of open range, and the fiction of the cowboy,
though much of it is laid outside of the Texas borders, has
a Texas tang that is inescapable. The Montana cowboy
was a legitimate copy of the Texas cowboy, but he was
just that, a copy of the original. Such middle and northern
chroniclers as Granville Stuart, E. C. Abbott, John Clay,
and the dean of them all, Joseph G. McCoy, testified on
more than one occasion that the cattlemen's frontier was
a Texas story from beginning to end. So Texans it was,
men a generation removed from the glories of the Alamo
and San Jacinto, and Texans it will have to be, as the tale
is spun of these trail drivers who replaced the buffalo with
cattle and traded the Indian yell for the folk ballad and
religious hymn, as the bow and arrow and tomahawk gave
way to the plow.

Like any giant undertaking, a trail drive didn't just
happen, but in a lesser way required the kind of organization, not to mention imagination coupled with devotion to
detail, that goes into staging a military operation. In the
spring, the prospective drover, who might be a rancher
ranging thousands of acres or just some buyer starting on
a shoestring without a square foot of land of his own,
would begin to gather a quota of steers. If he were pur-
chasing, he would probably make a round of ranches, buy-

ing and obtaining agreements to have the cattle delivered to a certain place where the herd would be made up. The cattle would be bought at so much a head, with the same price being paid for each, regardless of age or condition or weight, most weights being "guessed off" in those days. When the cattle had been received at their agreed-on point, they would be run through a chute and road branded to show a change of ownership and thereby to prevent misunderstandings up the trail.[1]

Meanwhile the drover had employed trail bosses to take charge of the individual herds so long as they were on the trail. Pointing the herds any number of possible places—Dodge City, Ogallala, or the Yellowstone River on the northern plains, he would give his boss either cash or a letter of credit and send him on his way with instructions for delivery. By wage standards of the time, a competent trail boss came high, usually drawing down about 125 dollars a month; but it was money well spent, for the boss was not only a foreman but really a sort of military field commander in charge of men and material—material which could represent an investment as high as 100,000 dollars.[2] The trail-boss class of Texans became one of the finest representative groups in the state.

The cowboys working under the trail boss tended to be young, not infrequently in their late teens or early twenties. Two things they all knew—how to ride and the technique of handling wild cattle. Especially they knew how to ride. Tommy Tucker says they "rode the wild hosses when they were drunk, and they rode them when they were sober, but no old-time cowpoke got up with his hands full of dust." [3] Occasionally one of them would be a Negro, or again a Mexican, though most Texans disliked

[1] John Marvin Hunter, *The Trail Drivers of Texas,* 21.
[2] Dale, *The Range Cattle Industry,* 65.
[3] Patrick T. Tucker, *Riding the High Country,* 128.

the latter, no matter how good riders they might be, as they would work for less money than the twenty-five to forty dollars a month which the cowboy asked for.

The trail boss might run the outfit, but on the trail it was the cook who needed to be humored. His was no easy job, working anywhere from three o'clock in the morning till perhaps midnight, always in the vanguard of the herd. Next to the trail boss, he was the highest paid hand. He was also likely to be the most exposed to Indians, for there would be times when he would be a mile or more ahead of the herd and its armed cowboys.[4] Sated with adventure, he was the realist of the crew who knew that, though the West might offer mystery, on the long haul food came first, and that he had better ration his stock of groceries to last out the trip. In addition, he was the storekeeper, looking after blankets, saddles, bridles, and other such supplies.

As a rule, the food the cook set out was uninspired. First of all his larder had to be portable, and it had to keep through any sort of weather. Accordingly he stocked up on corn meal, sorghum molasses, beans, salt, and mast-fed bacon.[5] Occasionally the diet would be varied by slaughtering a beef, or by killing a buffalo or deer. "Teddy Blue" Abbott claimed that one reason so many Texas cowboys went north and stayed there was because they were tired of cornbread and sowbelly.

The other member of the trail outfit was the horse wrangler, whose business it was to take care of the "remuda," "saddle band," or "caballado," as the riding stock were variously called, and the paraphernalia which went with the stock. Usually the wrangler was a boy old enough to work like a man. Thus "Little Joe, the wrangler," who

[4] James H. Cook, "The Texas Trail," *Nebraska History Magazine*, Vol. XVI, No. 4 (October–December, 1937), 237–38.
[5] Granville Stuart, *Forty Years on the Frontier*, II, 189.

never saw his mother in the fall. Sizes of *remudas* varied from six mounts to a man to the two that Charles Goodnight, pioneer Texas Panhandle ranchman, claimed were sufficient. A man's best mount was his night horse, and was never to be used for any other purpose. The other horses were to be used in rotation until each had been worked.[6] A *remuda* might easily total sixty-five to one hundred or more horses.

There's no end of descriptions of the herd on the trail, for it was a sight to burn deep into a man's memory; to rank, in earlier times, with an armada of sailing ships strung out stern-to-bow as far as the horizon would let the eye see, or in more modern times, with the *peregrinaciones* walking the two hundred miles from Queretaro to the Shrine of Guadalupe in Mexico, or with the American fleet filing out of Ulithi lagoon heading for Okinawa, or even with the tourists trailing single-file down into Carlsbad Caverns. "Gaunt, dust-caked, nervous longhorns coming over a rise . . . with dilated nostrils eagerly twitching for the smell of water" formed a narrow serpentine line stretching beyond the visible curvature of the earth; a massed group whose horns were constantly striking together with sharp, popping noises which, played against the beat of thousands of hoofs, produced a rhythmic dissonance as impelling—and almost as disquieting—as a bolero—the effect on viewer and auditor was invariably thrilling, and to the uninitiated, frightening.[7]

At a given moment it could sometimes seem as if the whole Western world had been taken over by the longhorn. E. C. Abbott, who among other things was Granville Stuart's son-in-law, recalled such a moment in 1883. Coming over a rise near the North Platte looking for strays, he

[6] Hunter, *The Trail Drivers of Texas*, 859. *Prose and Poetry*, 532.
[7] Denhardt, *The Horse of the Americas*, 176.

saw seven trail herds grazing behind his cattle, and eight more herds immediately ahead, while across the river he could see the trail dust of thirteen other herds. All the cattle in the world, he remarked, seemed to be coming up out of Texas that year.[8]

Like men, longhorns had their individualities, if not souls of their own, and like men, they had diverse temperaments and differed in their capacities to lead, to follow, and to behave. A few would take the lead at the outset of the journey and would keep it during the entire journey. And one stout old range steer would assert his authority as the monarch of the drive. Others occupied a middle position, important middlemen in the principal part of the herd, and like men, of course, there were the stragglers who made up the "drag," dragging out of the live-oak country of Texas and dragging into Kansas, apparently as determined to keep their position in the wake of the herd as the monarch was to keep his lead.

The cowboys rode in definite positions in relation to the cattle strung out along the trail for perhaps a half mile or more. Two cowboys, known as "pointers," rode in the lead or "point" at the head of the herd. These posts of honor were always occupied by the experienced riders whose duty it was to direct the herd, to prevent mix-ups with other herds on the trail, and to head off threatened stampedes. The cowboy on the left point was next in command to the trail boss. At an appropriate distance behind the pointers followed the "swing riders," followed in turn by the "flank riders." The rear was brought up by the "drag riders," whose business it was to look out for the calves, the played out, the sorefooted, and the lazy laggards. The poorest hands usually worked the drag, be-

[8] E. C. Abbott and Helena Huntington Smith, *We Pointed Them North*, 77.

cause no first-class cowboy would accept a position nursing a bunch of unwilling or unfit cattle while choking on the dust of a whole herd. If an experienced cowboy hired out to a trail outfit and found himself assigned to the drag, the likelihood was that the outfit would find itself minus one hand almost immediately.[9]

The responsibility for the safety and the delivery of the trail herd belonged entirely to the trail boss. His tasks on the trail were many and his judgment had to be good. The foremen had to know a day ahead of time where water could be found. When a new trail was to be laid out for the next day, the trail boss would be up at daybreak, prospecting fifteen or twenty miles ahead to locate desirable watering and camping sites. When he returned from his scouting trip, he would mount a rise of ground in full view of the herd, ride briskly around in a broad circle, and then would turn his horse broadside to the herd, which was the signal to drive ahead. If he wished the direction of the trail herd to be changed, he would ride to a new point and again turn his horse broadside. The trail boss also used his hat for a kind of sign language borrowed from the Plains Indians. Generally he carried a compass, but when he did not, the wagon tongue was pointed at night at the North Star, and the journey was resumed the next morning accordingly.[10]

Although the trail drives were never without their problems, the drives could be accomplished with reasonable certainty. A day's drive generally averaged about ten miles, the distance always being determined by the water and grass supply. The trail boss would push the cattle for the first three or four days, traveling between twenty-five

[9] Stuart, *Forty Years*, II, 189. Abbott and Smith, *We Pointed Them North*, 74.

[10] *Prose and Poetry*, 543–45. Webb, *The Great Plains*, 265. Hunter, *The Trail Drivers of Texas*, 368.

and thirty miles each day. But as soon as the cattle were driven from their home range, they were slowed down to an average of eight or ten miles a day, which didn't represent much more daily range than they would cover at home. The riders kept the cattle in formation on the trail by riding from their position rearward and pressing in toward the center, thereby overcoming the tendency of the stock to spread out. When they met the drivers to the immediate rear, the front riders would turn, swing boldly from the herd, and ride back in a more distant line to repeat the maneuver. In this way, a line of cattle two or three miles in length could be held in a compact line, and herds which left Texas as a fractious, undisciplined lot usually would become quite tractable as the drive progressed.[11]

In the main, each day's drive was repeated in a pattern that soon became automatic. Early in the morning the cowboys would start the cattle moving, working them into a tenuous thread with one side of the cordon relaxed to permit controlled grazing in a desired direction. For three or four miles the cattle would graze along, after which they would be trailed steadily for another three or four miles. After nooning and, if possible, watering, the cattle would graze on till near sundown. Meanwhile the cook would have pulled ahead to make camp at a bedding ground, preferably one with plenty of water, and the herd would be timed to graze into the camping area before darkness set in. Bedding the herd was accomplished by the cowboys' circling and continually contracting the circuit until the cattle were moved into a compact enough body to lie down. The cattle would lie quietly until about

[11] Stuart, *Forty Years*, II, 192. James Cox, *Historical and Biographical Record of the Cattle Industry and the Cattlemen of Texas*, 191. Cook, "The Texas Trail," *Nebraska History Magazine*, Vol. XVI, No. 4 (October–December, 1937), 231.

eleven o'clock, when a stir would be heard as they rose to lie down in a new position. A short distance away the riders' horses would be hobbled, while one cowboy kept watch over the horses as part of his guard duty.

With the longhorns bedded down for the night, four night watches would be set, the first till ten o'clock, the second till midnight, the third till two o'clock, and the last till morning. Morning was greeted with some ceremony, as cowboys on watch undoubtedly took the same slightly sadistic satisfaction in rousing a sleeping camp that sentries display in a military camp—a sort of "If I can't sleep, neither is any other son-of-a-whatever going to either!"

> "The bulls are in the pen!
> Arise and shine!
> Give God the glory!"

But don't be so loudmouthed about it that you'll startle the cattle—"one jump to their feet and the second jump to hell!" [12]

With the horses unhobbled and with breakfast in the cowboys' lean bellies, the trail riders would begin the gradual moving of the herd. From then on, the remainder of the day followed the familiar pattern, except the pattern was liable to change at a moment's notice. There was no telling what sudden noise might "stompead" the herd, or when. S. H. Wood, a trail driver, told of some fifty herds of longhorns grazing along the Arkansas River outside Dodge City when a thunderstorm struck. It was a week before the herds were back in place.[13] While some cattle became sick and died, others became too footsore to continue. And Indians exacted their toll. The result was

[12] Stuart, *Forty Years*, II, 189–190. Cook, "The Texas Trail," *Nebraska History Magazine*, Vol. XVI, No. 4 (October–December, 1937), 235. Dobie, *A Vaquero of the Brush Country*, 96.
[13] Hunter, *The Trail Drivers of Texas*, 170.

that a recount of the herd while it was trailing was always in order; this was accomplished by driving the herd between two hands, each keeping his own tally and then checking and reconciling with the other when the count was complete.[14]

The most feared experience on the trail, which was not too serious a problem on the road to Kansas, but which was ever-present in drives through West Texas and the Panhandle, was the long drive without water. Charles Goodnight describes such a drive that he made across the Staked Plains—the Llano Estacado—from the headwaters of the South Concho to the Pecos, a punishing drive under the most favorable conditions. The cattle were watered and grazed at the Concho about noon, then marched briskly till midnight, when they were permitted to graze again while the hands ate. That done, the herd was put again on the trail and kept moving till daylight, when another brief stop was made for breakfast. Before noon, the herd was moving so fast it had to be slowed for the weaker cattle.

By daylight of the second morning, the herd would be within ten or twelve miles—smelling distance, if the wind were right—of the Pecos, when care had to be redoubled, for if the cattle did smell the water, they would likely stampede for the river, killing and maiming as they went. And even beyond the Pecos, there remained the possibility for another dozen miles that the cattle might turn to rush back to the water they had left behind.[15]

Andy Adams ran into such an experience once, the heat-crazed cattle turning back despite every device to halt them, even to discharging six-shooters point blank into the faces of the lead steers. In a number of instances

[14] *Ibid.*, 232–34.
[15] *Prose and Poetry*, 536.

steers walked deliberately into the side of the horses, when "for the first time a fact dawned on us that chilled the marrow in our bones,—*the herd was going blind*." [16]

A calculated risk, but no more pleasant for its deliberateness, arose from swimming the great trail herds across the rivers, especially in the spring, when the rivers, ordinarily as smooth as a baseball infield for three-quarters of a year, could rampage beyond all control. Like the first Western railroads, the rivers ran horizontally across the plains, so that trail drivers had to follow the lines of most resistance: their journeys northward ran athwart the swollen streams. Depending on where the herd was assembled, a drive could cross all of the major rivers—the Colorado, Brazos, and Red in Texas; the Canadian, North Canadian, and Cimarron in the Indian country; the Arkansas in Kansas; and if headed for Ogallala, the North Platte in Nebraska. Other trails had their crossing problems also, ranging from the Pecos in the West to the Stinkingwater in Montana.

The herding, by twelve men on horseback, of three thousand half-wild, nervous longhorns down high banks and across rivers washed by swift spring floods called for an operation that even in the comfort of a TV lounge seems well-nigh impossible. The crossing was planned with the care of a marine amphibious landing. The jumping-off area was combed for the most likely staging spot, the trail boss swam the river with an eye for sink holes and quicksand, and a landing place was chosen that would insure quick ascent of the opposite heights, and which at the same time would be far enough downstream to allow for the cattle to drift with the current, not to mention the fact that even in a still pond cattle can't swim in a straight line. The groundwork laid, the point riders, accompanied by their

[16] Adams, *The Log of a Cowboy*, 63-64.

top sergeant—a proud old steer born to lead—would plunge into the water, hoping for the best but depending on vigilance and skill more than on hope.

In the water the cattle would form a giant, incomplete U as a result of their drifting. The cowboys, largely naked, would ride below the cattle to keep the herd from swimming with the current beyond the landing site. Any minute any number of things could go wrong. The herd could begin to mill in midstream, drowning those to the center. Jack Abernathy, the wolf wrestler, tells how on one crossing the A-K-X cattle massed so closely that the herd boss in a desperate effort to loosen the tangle jumped from his horse to the backs of the cattle and "running, cursing and firing his pistol rapidly," crossed the entire herd without ever getting back down. The herd might miss the selected landing and emerge to face sheer banks, or the lead steer might decide not to enter the stream, or, once in, turn back. And if the herd turned, anything could be expected. Cattle would not swim if they could not see the opposite bank; neither would they swim with the sun in their eyes. Many attempts might have to be made before the longhorns would finally be put across.[17]

Crossing the *remuda* was accomplished in the same manner, but without the accompanying danger. In the absence of ferries, crossing the chuck wagon might require repeated trips. It could be dismantled and floated across on improvised rafts, while individual cowboys lashed meal and coffee to their horses' backs and swam over the supplies. Whenever possible, the chuck wagon was sent in advance of the herd so that hot food could be served after the crossing.[18]

[17] Stuart, *Forty Years*, II, 192. Adams, *The Log of a Cowboy*, 106. John R. Abernathy, *In Camp with Theodore Roosevelt*, 31–32.
[18] Cook, "The Texas Trail," *Nebraska History Magazine*, Vol. XVI, No. 4 (October–December, 1937), 238.

Cowboys loved their work, but as none of them appreciated a crossing till it was successfully concluded, the river became as real an enemy as the Mississippi is to the delta sharecropper. Of the Red, Andy Adams remarked, "she was merciless, . . . for although this crossing had been in use only a year or two when we forded, yet five graves, one of which was less than ten days made, attested her disregard for human life." [19]

And so the trail days would go by, and the cattle would move ten miles closer to market at the end of each of the days. Most of the time it was dull work, lonely work, dirty work, and hungry work, helped along only by the fact that men drew close to each other from the constant, enforced companionship, by the prospect of a hell-raisin' time in Dodge City, by the growing *esprit* of an outfit—the same spirit that invests the crew of a destroyer who, though admittedly they may hate the guts of every other crewman aboard, want to fight anybody else who won't admit that theirs is the "best stinkin' barge" afloat—and by the possibility that routine might be sharply punctured any moment by some round-eyed steer clambering to his feet and taking off, with the whole herd hot behind him.

Ninety days it took to get from San Antonio to Abilene —five weeks from the Red River to the Kansas border— six months from Texas to the High Plains. Days and weeks and months of snailing along a trail whose sides raveled out like the strands of a torn rope or a piece of unhemmed burlap, a trail anywhere from fifty yards to two miles wide, a chocolate band threaded across a green prairie, a trail without soil, pushed lower than the surrounding country by the seemingly ceaseless pounding of thousands of sharp hoofs, flanked by little banks of sand drifted by the wind, and marked by the bleached skull of an animal,

[19] *The Log of a Cowboy*, 121.

the occasional grave of a cowhand who never would shoot up Abilene again, a dilapidated wagon frame beyond going on, or the barren circle of a bedding ground telling that a herd had stopped here the night before. Here along these trails passed the wealth of an empire.[20]

There were other trails to other places. The northern trails leading out of Montana and Wyoming have their epic stories, too. The so-called transcontinental railroads roared through and past, seldom stopping, since to stop in a country in which there was only grass and desert would have been, as one observer noted, "fatal, because there was nothing to stop for." [21] It was the northern cowboy who conquered and colonized that void which the railroads at first were inclined to pass over, paving the way for the farmer with his barbed wire and windmills, just as his Texas cousin did to the south. But it is the trails out of the south that fixed the cowboy in the American imagination, the trails from Texas to Abilene and Dodge City. Without the Chisholm Trail, without the Western Trail, the American cowboy might never have emerged as a hero of fiction and folklore and balladry. If the place setting of the cowboy can be narrowed to two locales, those locales belong to the trails from Texas and to the little frontier towns lined across that gritty ironing board known as Kansas. The trail gave the cowboy the stature of a heroic frontiersman; the cowtown at the end of the trail gave him a bad reputation which in the long run brought him as much fame and appreciation as his more heroic qualities. The trail, the town, and the cowboy are inseparable.

[20] Sam R. Riding, *The Chisholm Trail*, 15. Charles Moreau Harger, "Cattle-Trails of the Prairies," *Scribner's Magazine*, Vol. XI (1892), 734. Stuart Henry, *Conquering Our Great American Plains*, 40–42.
  [21] Webb, *The Great Plains*, 274.

4. The Ranch and the Range

ALTHOUGH the Texas trail drives on the Chisholm and Western trails form the foundation for the whole structure of what Walter Prescott Webb called "the most unique and distinctive institution that America has produced," and a large part of the cowboy folk material has its origin in those drives, the spread of the longhorns into the northern plains and the utilization of all of the Great Plains for immense grazing grounds fashioned the historical materials for much of Western fiction.[1] The trail drives are a Texas story, but the range cattle industry be-

[1] *The Great Plains,* 224.

48

longs to all the West, and names like Arizona and Wyoming have as much historical legitimacy and as much artistic appeal for writers as Texas and Chisholm any day, while the plains of Colorado, Wyoming, Montana, and the Dakotas, flanked by the Rocky Mountains, have a beauty and romance which the harsh, flat southern reaches of the plains can never possess. If the cowboy won his national fame on the trails and in the Kansas cowtowns, the range and ranch frontier provided him with respectability and made him an admirably romantic American folk type.

If the western part of the United States had been as wooded and well watered as the country east of the Mississippi, it is unlikely that such a person as the cowboy would have emerged. But the Great Plains presented a problem unlike anything hitherto challenging the American in his westward questing. When he first came upon the plains stretching almost limitlessly to the horizon in waving rolls of green grass, broken only here and there by islands of shrubbery and scrub trees, occasionally cut by a small stream straggling its way across the green swells, the Anglo-American saw a region beyond his personal or ancestral experience. He saw a land of little rain and of mighty distances which was going to humble him and teach him before he would fashion new tools to cope with the new environment. He saw a land which though pleasant and gracious to look upon was going to remain raw and mean to live with till the turn of the century and after. It's a land that in 1955 is still never easy.

As 1870 came on, it was not unknown for eastern passengers on the new Union Pacific to see from their train windows a herd of buffalo or a band of hostile Indians or a Texas trail herd strung out sinuously across the plain, or to ride with a group of genuine frontier cowboys taking the train for the long trip back to Texas. No period in American history brought such complete and sharply contrasting contact between civilization and savagery as the general period during which the cattlemen's frontier was being extended on the northern plains.[2]

The northern plains and the Rocky Mountains were regions not entirely unknown to the Anglo-American. In the first years of the nineteenth century, the mountain men, later typified by Kit Carson, had gone into the Rockies to trap beaver and had been permitted by the Indians to live peacefully. After 1849 had come the miners. In the latter 1860's, the Union Pacific pushed its way across plains and mountains.

But as late as 1870, the major portion of the Great Plains was still unsettled and unclaimed, from western Kansas to the Sierra Nevadas, and from the Red River to Canada. Hardly a white man lived in the western half of Texas. These were the lands that constituted the public domain in 1870, and these were the areas which the frontier rancher was appropriating as free range for grazing his millions of cattle and sheep. Within fifteen years these areas had become one vast pastoral dominion. And unlike the gold washer and the buffalo hunter, the men who trailed the herds of longhorns onto the plains came to make their homes.

A number of considerations led to the extension of the cattlemen's frontier to the upper and outer reaches of the Great Plains. First of all, extreme weather and limited grazing grounds were not as forbidding as at first supposed. Even before the Civil War, it had been found that the northern ranges were ideal for pasturing stock. For five hundred miles eastward from the Rockies, fine velvety sky-bluish buffalo grass grew three or four inches tall in

[2] Ernest Staples Osgood, *The Day of the Cattleman*, 59.

Erwin E. Smith: Library of Congress

DEW ON THE GRASS. The drag end of the trail herd
could be pleasant, but wait . . .

Erwin E. Smith: Library of Congress

BONE DRY ON THE TRAIL. This is what the
men in the drags saw as the day lengthened.

the spring, only to cure on the stem when summer came, but retaining all of its nutritious qualities nonetheless.[3] Because railroad crews needed fresh meat and because hide hunters had a market, the bison were decimated, leaving their grazing ground for domesticated cattle. Tales of profit in Texas cattle led northern men to seek extension of the cattle-raising area to their ranges. And the gradual subjugation of the Indians provided still greater grazing area.

The beginning of the cattle business on the High Plains goes back to the immigrants passing over the Oregon Trail before the Civil War. Mountain men caught by the end of the fur-trade boom observed immigrant cattle becoming lame and footsore, and set out to provide fresh animals. Before long, the mountain men were small-scale cattlemen, owning modest herds and trading with regularity. Furthermore, the "bull teams" of Russell, Majors, and Waddell, who supplied frontier army posts, mining camps, and Indian annuity goods, had to be wintered along the trail. The winter of 1857–1858 saw the freighting firm wintering 15,000 head. Still other cattle were brought in by miners.

These were only beginnings. Not till the Union Pacific penetrated the borders of Wyoming in 1867 did the northern plains begin to realize their potential for developing and stocking the empty ranges with cattle. By 1869, Colorado, the first state really to feel the impact of the Texas invasion, was grazing a million cattle and twice as many sheep within its borders. By then Wyoming had connected with Texas through John W. Iliff, first of the northern cattle kings, who had met Charles Goodnight in New Mexico, purchased the Texan's herd, and driven it to the Cheyenne

[3] Cox, *Historical and Biographical Record,* 34.

vicinity in February, 1868, where he was soon selling beef to local dealers for five cents a pound.[4]

In that same year, the Union Pacific began the circulation of an apocryphal story of a government trader en route to Utah who, caught by an unusually severe storm on the Laramie plains, turned his cattle loose to perish from starvation and cold. But instead, as the snow was blown off the high lands, the dry grass afforded abundant forage, so that spring found the cattle in better condition than when they had been turned loose. Such a story need not be true (and there are several versions), for it was sufficient that such environmental conditions were credible and verifiable. Winter grazing in the northern plains area soon became one of the marvels of the period, and the cattle industry, surging with confidence, began to move inexorably northward until finally, in 1879, one hundred thousand Texas longhorns were trailed into Montana to establish that cold country just below the Canadian border permanently as a cattle region.[5]

The last region to fill with cattle was Arizona, which developed late as a beef-producing area because of its distance from market, the tardy arrival of railroads, and the delayed dispatching of Geronimo and other Apaches. When the railroads finally came in 1880 and 1881, they opened a virtually virgin area to eager capitalists, both American and foreign, who invested so fast that they soon overcrowded the range, destroyed the grass, and lowered the quality of Arizona beef. But Arizona has the same mild weather as Texas, plus great natural charm, so that the men who came decided to remain and to work out their problems of overstocking, which they managed to do with such effectiveness that today Arizona comes to mind as

[4] Osgood, *The Day of the Cattleman*, 9–10, 16–17, 43.
[5] *Ibid.*, 87.

quickly as Texas when cattle ranching is mentioned. Arizona, in fact, with its mountains and Indians and painted deserts is easily the favorite setting for contemporary cowboy fiction.

Extension of the cattlemen's frontier throughout the Great Plains is rather a repetitious story, and the methods of handling cattle differed little from one region to another. But because it is a story that proceeds according to formula, the extension of cattle ranching over hundreds of thousands of acres in the West—a story which in men and money and acreage involved, should dwarf the trail drives of Texas—nonetheless lacks the thrill and adventure of trail driving days. Actually, frontier trailing and frontier ranching were complementary, but it was the old-time trail drivers who supplied the basic myths and the local color for the cattleman's frontier. Here, however, the fiction writer unconsciously has moved closer to reality by fusing the two processes regardless of what the historian may tell him of their separateness. One error the fiction-monger does persist in, though, is in insisting on laying his plots in or near well-established frontier towns which as a rule simply did not exist. But perhaps such error only perpetuates and enlarges the myth, as there is no rule that a myth must withstand close analysis of its validity.

Whenever men organize in any great undertaking, a social and cultural pattern will develop as a consequence. Thus ranching on the plains, a business proposition designed to show a profit, developed an almost scientific rigidity in its approach to its problems, while at the same time it injected elements essential to the cowboy myth as we know it today. For instance, the trail had no room for the feminine element, though Hough did include such an element in his *North of 36*, to the distaste of a host of otherwise wholehearted worshipers. Women did come to the ranches. Furthermore, there was an inherent dramatic quality in the shortness of the frontier ranching period which made for conflict, that greatest of boons to the teller of tales. In hardly more than a half-dozen hectic years— years in which one man's right to grass and water was as good as another's, if he could make it stick—capitalists perceived investment opportunity, realized the millions of acres of grass available almost for the taking, imagined the fabulous profits, and foresaw that a government histori- cally generous with the public domain could not much longer exercise that largess. The scramble took place mainly between 1879 and 1885, less than a third of the time occupied by the trailing chapter. The rancher of the 1870's, supreme in, and enjoying fully, his isolation, and the hemmed-in rancher of the late 1880's, who realized now that God hadn't made the Great Plains solely for his exploitation, were two entirely different types, a fact yet to be learned by most practitioners in Western fiction.

How did one become a frontier rancher? He found a live stream with an ample supply of water and established a headquarters camp at a desirable adjacent spot. If trees could be found, so much the better. Then he could claim all of the land facing the stream for fifteen or twenty miles, and backed up from the stream as far as the water divide. Beyond the divide lay the land of another rancher. If a rancher claimed both sides of the stream, he would claim to the water divide on both sides. If he were in an area without streams, but with a waterhole as the only water- ing facility within miles, he could select his homestead about the hole, and with the backing of federal land laws control all the surrounding ranges as effectively as if they were enclosed.[6] The principle for the division of free lands

[6] Webb, *The Great Plains*, 229. Osgood, *The Day of the Cattleman*, 184.

was that uninvolved, though revolver and rifle might be necessary adjuncts to principle.

Housing was simple because it was perforce crude. A "house" might be a dugout in the side of a bank, with a roof covered with logs and an overlay of prairie sod, or two rooms with a chimney, the outside of lumber, logs, or adobe, depending on the availability of material. The "nest-building of the Texan," opined one mid-1880's novelist, "is not characterized by [an] air of luxurious refinement." On the northern plains, a house might be made of cottonwood logs chinked with mud and moss and a roof of dirt and branches. A door could be made of dried beef hide, a bed of wolf hides (fleas might be annoying at first, but fleas soon leave a dead hide, which comes under the head of truly worthwhile information!), and seats of buffalo skulls.[7] This was home, the place from which to create a cattle barony. This was not the pleasant ranch headquarters pictured by writers and movie producers.

In time, ranching facilities caught up with continued business success. Goodnight's JA Ranch home was a two-story plank-and-log structure with water piped in from a large spring a thousand yards above the house. There was a separate mess house for the men, along with a blacksmith shop, dairy, poultry yard, and other outbuildings.[8] But in the early stages the ranch headquarters was more habitation than real home, beyond the reach of close neighbors, beyond the reach of mail delivery, beyond the reach of city facilities, and almost beyond reach.

Ranching, of course, had an entirely different purpose from trailing. The range and ranches were established for

[7] Everett Dick, *The Sod House Frontier*, 113–15. Carl Coke Rister, *The Southwestern Frontier, 1865–1881*, 254–55. Roosevelt, *Ranch Life and the Hunting Trail*, 7. Howard Seely, *A Lone Star Bo-Peep*, 28. William Curry Holden, *Rollie Burns*, 79.

[8] J. Evetts Haley, *Charles Goodnight, Cowman and Plainsman*, 327–28.

increasing herds and for fattening cattle for market, while trailing was concerned with getting herds to market, or with conquering a transportation problem which was solved by the ability of the longhorns to move anywhere across the plains. Unlike trailing, then, the ranching industry before barbed wire was concerned about how to keep cattle on the home range. In the absence of fences, a human fence was erected, in effect, with so-called "line riders" patrolling ceaselessly the boundaries of the ranch to maintain ownership and possession of herds against such diverse incursions as Indians, thieves, wild animals, and disease. Beyond the reach of local government also, it was the responsibility of the individual ranch to see after its own security, though shortly, of course, as ranches grew more numerous and correspondingly drew closer together, ranchers' associations would provide aid.[9]

It is hardly necessary to say anything about the semi-annual roundups, when the cattle were either branded for identification or were cut out for any number of reasons—because they were scrubs or were diseased perhaps. From a strictly man-versus-steer standpoint, the roundup required more varied skill and ranching knowledgeability than trailing, but since fiction writers and their Tin Pan Alley colleagues have discovered the roundup in force, a detailed account of it can be omitted here. Roundups were a necessary business practice—or a prelude to business practice; they were a time of hard work, intermingled with dirt and heat and the acrid smell of burning hair and flesh and the bawling of outraged "cows" (for in truth all bovines, regardless of sex or outlook, were cows to the cowboy); and they were a social time too, not entirely unrelated to the old barn-raisings of Colonial days.

With the new prosperity which the range cattle indus-

[9] Osgood, *The Day of the Cattleman,* 28–29.

try brought from Texas northward, there came a rush of men to enter the business, legitimately or otherwise, with the further result that soon organization became necessary to determine strict ownership, even to the hiring of stock detectives. These formal organizations, themselves a nail in the coffin of free pasturage and open range, protected property against theft, regulated brands and other marks, set up controls for water and grasslands, and established a roundup system designed to prevent overworking the ranges by different owners at different times.[10]

As state and territorial associations grew in size and power, they divided the West into roundup districts, and roundups became distinctly collaborative ventures. Custom was to send word to all of the ranchmen in an area announcing date and place. Usually eight or ten ranches would be represented at the ensuing roundup. The larger outfits would bring their own chuck wagons, with the smaller ranches paying a nominal fee for the privilege of eating someone else's chuck. While preliminary preparations were being made at the site, the men would occupy themselves by overhauling their gear and holding a reunion. There were the inevitable card games, some frolicking, and occasional hilarious—to the cowboys—kangaroo courts built around ridiculous charges. At a really large roundup, as many as two hundred and fifty to three hundred men might turn up, though the more likely number was somewhat fewer than a hundred. Some of the men might be ranchers from other districts on hand to check whether any cattle might have strayed beyond the local district's bounds.[11]

Roundups could be enormous affairs, especially on the northern ranges, sometimes covering a range the size of

[10] *Ibid.*, 131.
[11] *Prose and Poetry*, 609–611. Hunter, *The Trail Drivers of Texas*, 344–45. Dale, *The Range Cattle Industry*, 100.

Connecticut and involving several thousand cattle. To supervise, the association named a roundup judge to see that the associational rules were followed and invested him with all the authority of a major league baseball umpire. On a typical roundup, on the evening before, three men from each outfit would be chosen to ride out from the camp in all directions for fifteen or twenty miles to make a dry camp. When morning came, the men would then begin to ride toward the center grounds driving the cattle before them. Constantly they narrowed the circumference of the circle of cattle, converging steadily toward the center of the web. A stray steer had scant chance of getting by, for if he worked away from one rider, he most likely would drift into the sweep of another rider. And as the web tightened, the number of men at hand increased. Finally one great herd would be formed at the center, and the branding operation could begin.[12]

The work of a roundup consisted of separating the animals into lesser herds according to individual owners, branding the calves, castrating them, and so on. The sorting out, or "cutting," of cattle called for bold and skillful horsemanship, and today is still one of the more attractive features of cowboy life, as far as illustrating the oneness of instinct and action which a man and his mount can achieve. As the cattle were collected by brands, they were kept in groups a mile apart, where some men tended the fire and others applied the red-hot irons. Calves were identified by their mothers, who never failed to know their own. Work on the range was continued until it was cleaned of cattle, after which the outfits would break up, most of them returning to their individual sites, a few perhaps going to a contiguous district for whatever cattle they

[12] *Prose and Poetry*, 609. Dale, *The Range Cattle Industry*, 100. Hunter, *The Trail Drivers of Texas*, 345.

might have there. On the whole, the great roundups were conducted in a spirit of fairness and camaraderie, and with a feeling for property rights.

Open range roundups lasted but a decade. After the middle eighties, barbed wire had become so common that the great roundups, like the great trail drives, were drifting fast into memory. With wire fences, the line rider became a fence rider.[13] Branding and roundups continue, but for sixty-five years they have been more of a preventive measure against rustling and a compliance with demands of legal ownership than a method for establishing ownership among cattle on the open range. In both eras, ranch hands lived a hard occupational life. Whatever glamor may have been associated with their work was based on skills attained only after long and often dangerous apprenticeship. Fred Gipson gives a picture of his cowhand friend Fat Alford, a 1950 cowboy but a cowboy who, with slight alteration, would fit the picture of the proper cowboy in any age. Alford, says Gipson, by Hollywood standards "is a far cry from being a typical cowhand. He never shot a man in his life. He never chased a rustler across the Rio Grande. He never rescued a beautiful girl from ruthless bandits and rode off into the sunset with his arm about her waist." But, Gipson goes on:

He can rope a cow out of a brush patch so thick that a Hollywood cowboy couldn't crawl into it on his hands and knees. He can break a horse for riding, doctor a wormy sheep, make a balky gasoline engine pump water for thirsty cattle, tail up a winter-poor cow, or punch a string of post holes across a rocky ridge. He can make out with patched gear, sorry mounts, and skimpy grub, and still get the job done. He can do it in freezing weather or under a sun "hot enough to raise blisters on a boot heel." And all the time, under any circumstances,

[13] *Prose and Poetry,* 614–17.

he works with the thorough understanding that it's the live-stock that counts, not the cowhand.

On top of all this, he's got a quality common to most working cowhands: a way of meeting life head on, with a recklessness and a wildness of spirit and a real relish for conquering it. He goes after life as if it were something that had to be roped in a hurry before it got away. And whether he catches it or not, it's a good chase, worth the try, and will make an entertaining yarn. . . .[14]

Such is, and was, the ranch cowboy. Today he may use a hay loader and stacker to replace old-time muscle and sweat, he may receive his hot meals by pickup truck from a ranch house twenty miles away, he may run a tractor and cable to clear brush out of a pasture, he may burn butane to heat his branding irons, he may use a jeep to haze his little dogies back into the yard, he may ride fence with an airplane, and he may let Bing Crosby croon to his cattle by radio rather than sing off-key and off-melody himself in the old-time fashion; but he remains a skilled worker of cattle, changed only by adapting to the technological revolution which eventually reached the range. He may not get on a horse in a week, but he is still a cowboy. And as a cowboy, he remains an object of glamor to many, though his actual chores may be no more glamorous than that of any South Bend lathe worker or Alabama field hand.

And, to be historically accurate, neither were the chores of the old-time cowhand especially glamorous. Certainly they weren't to him. And yet, still keeping an eye cocked on history, we must repeat that the cowboy, like his modern counterpart, was first of all a worker with cows. He was a man plying his trade, which happened to be trail driving or range riding, and not a gun-totin' half-

[14] *Cowhand,* v–vi.

alligator, half-man on a drunken spree in a red-light town. Not that he couldn't fill that role on occasion!

Although in many ways northern ranching outstrips Texas ranching, except in the story of trailing and for examples of individual bigness (as in the King, Three D, Matador, JA, and XIT ranches, for instances), even in ranching the Texas tone pervades regardless of location. The dyed-in-the-wool early cowboy was a Texan who had been reared on the open ranges, seemingly isolated from everything but horses and cattle. He knew the habits and customs of range cattle better than most men ever comprehend the habits of their wives. He had always lived on the frontier, and though he might collide with civilization occasionally, he always seemed a little surprised to discover its existence. He imposed his speech—or lingo—his dress, his actions, and his outlook on the whole range country, and his influence is still vitally alive in American folk life. Only technological advance improved his methods of handling cattle. His patience, ingenuity, faithfulness, loyalty, and alternating taciturnity and garrulity are legends.[15]

And the legends are not just in the United States. Take for example this account from an English magazine of the 1880's:

Cowboys can be divided into two classes: those hailing from the Lone Star State, Texas, the other recruited either from Eastern States, chiefly Missouri, or from the Pacific slopes; Oregon contributing no mean number of Webfoots, so called from the long winter rains in that colony. The Texans are, as far as true cowboyship goes, unrivalled: the best riders, hardy, and born to the business; the only drawback being their wild reputation. The others are less able but more orderly men. The

[15] Stuart, *Forty Years*, II, 182–83, 239. Roosevelt, *Ranch Life and the Hunting Trail*, 12–16. Abbott and Smith, *We Pointed Them North*, 3. C. L. Sonnichsen, *Cowboys and Cattle Kings*, 91–93.

bad name of Texans arises mostly from their excitable tempers, and the fact that they are mostly "on the shoot,"—that is, very free in the use of their revolvers.[16]

Frontier ranching naturally ran athwart the Indian problem in the West. The Indian was a problem in the Texas era, though a relatively straightforward one, and he was a considerably more complicated problem in the northern plains and in Arizona. The Indian problem worked both ways—in a sense it checked the development of the range cattle industry, while at the same time the insistence of the Western cattleman in following the grass and the streams helped to expedite the laying of the Indian threat. It is a considerable story, one over which writers have waxed indignant, over which anthropologists and apologists have wept copiously, and over which romanticists have grown enthusiastic. But it is a story for a later chapter, and so we will pass it here, merely pointing it out to show a perhaps skeptical reviewer that we were aware there was a relationship between the Indian and the rancher.

The Indian does serve to point up the fact that in many ways frontier ranching had an emphasis on survival, just as does most pioneer experience. But as usual, time supplanted survival emphasis with a pattern of improving existence. Permanent improvements were made, women came in, and refinements appeared. Englishmen were attracted to the cattle regions, and the English have a way of taking their particular culture with them into the most forbidding environment. (Roger Pocock's *Curly: A Story of the Arizona Desert*, telling of English aristocrats running cattle around Tombstone, has a valid historical base, whatever your opinion of the superstructure.) Men began

[16] W. Baillie Grohman, "Cattle Ranches in the Far West," *Fortnightly Review*, Vol. XXXIV (1880), 447.

to speak of "cattle barons" and "cattle kings," terms, or epithets, which Western cowmen shied away from, but names which indicate a certain arrival beyond the frontier stage.[17]

Still, by the very vastness of the ranching area involved, social life hardly existed. Mrs. Goodnight, one of the finest of frontier women, lived eight miles from her nearest woman neighbor and got to see her every six months. In most regions, a doctor, even at childbirth, was as undreamed of a luxury as the fabulous dinners Jim Fisk had been throwing back in New York until he got himself shot. When Hosburgh of the Spur ranch below Amarillo came down with pneumonia, a doctor had to be fetched all the way from Colorado at a cost of one hundred dollars. You might have to drink slick water with a green scum on it, but if you did, dismiss the possibility of consequent illness from your mind.[18] You couldn't afford to be ill; and if you did become ill, you couldn't afford a doctor, if you could locate one. A good midwife—or even a fat, greasy, complaining one—was hardly more likely to be available than a doctor. But somehow the women survived —in prairie schooners and dugouts, and then in crude cabins, and finally, if their men prospered, in a frame or stone house with a bit of comfort here and there. The country took its toll, for the women weathered quickly, and beauty and rosiness left the average ranch wife's face long before her chronological passing from young womanhood. When the movie fades out on wings of song and the first kiss, its maker shows his sagacity in sparing his audience, for the years ahead of the sweet young calicoed thing are likely to be grim and wearing and unrelieved.

As the country filled, the social tempo picked up and

[17] Cox, *Historical and Biographical Record*, 136.
[18] Haley, *Charles Goodnight*, 305. Holden, *Spur Ranch*, 104–105.

life lost some of its starkness. There were quilting parties, dances, taffy-pulls, weddings, picnics, and even funerals to break the monotony. Occasionally there was a camp meeting, as much social in its aspects as spiritual. The few womenfolk were likely to worry considerably about the unconcern of the average cowboy over his Eternal Life—not that the cowboy was antireligious, it just was seldom that church crossed his mind—and in some areas they tried to arrange missions, marked usually by a total lack of success. For their part, the men organized turkey and deer hunts, bronco breakings, and cutting horse contests. Most ranch owners discouraged their hands from marrying, an outlook which happily no longer prevails; and since there were considerably more men than women, the seamiest old crone could look good to most cowhands, while a decent enough looking woman was truly a prize. No woman was a wallflower at a dance, though it might have been safer to have graced the wall, for the cowboy whirling her so energetically might be bedecked in boots, Mexican spurs, sombrero, and revolver, not to mention the ever-present Levis with their copper-riveted pockets.[19]

Openhanded western hospitality was, and is, renowned, though with more reason in the 1880's. A stranger in a neighborhood was expected to visit every ranch before he headed back East. The best of everything—to which the supercilious might add in an aside, "such as it was"—was supposed to be trotted out for the visitor, and if the code was violated by some rancher who tried to get by with the second-best treatment, he was branded as socially despicable by his fellow ranchers and hands.

Between visits from the outside, or trailing cattle, or

[19] Henry, *Conquering Our Great American Plains*, 256. Roosevelt, *Ranch Life and the Hunting Trail*, 150–51. Rister, *Southwestern Frontier*, 259. Reginald Aldridge, *Ranch Notes*, 75–76. Sonnichsen, *Cowboys and Cattle Kings*, 96–97.

putting up hay for the horses, or rounding up cattle, or riding line, there wasn't much for the average cowboy to do, especially in the winter. Some of them lounged about the bunkhouse, or rode "the grub line" from ranch kitchen to ranch kitchen, or trapped wolves for bounty. Gambling usually was forbidden, though card games were tolerated. Some cowboys whiled away their time with a fiddle or guitar or mouth organ. Stewart Edward White tells how he spent his time looking up at his bunkhouse ceiling and counting bullet holes—3,620 of them—put there by bored cowboys shooting at flies overhead. The cowboy could indulge his sense of humor, which usually found its outlet in the exaggerated tale or in horseplay, as, for instance, when a group of cowpokes corralled the pet donkey of a Mrs. Gethings and sheared it like a French poodle.[20]

Small wonder then that the ranch hand was ready to blow the lid off a frontier town when he arrived with a couple hundred dollars in back pay. A hot bath, a haircut and shave, a hotel room with reasonably clean sheets—or just with sheets, stores full of new (and gaudy) clothes, and bars and dance halls and compliant women ready, for a drink or a price, to act as if you were the boldest and cleverest man who ever reeled into their lives. To the steady people in town, a cowboy on the loose was a menace, or at least a nuisance, but he had money to spend and steady people are in business for money. Sometimes the sprees would eventuate in Boot Hill cemetery, but why mourn the loss of a cowboy who, as the townspeople knew, was more mustang than man anyway?[21]

[20] Grohman, "Cattle Ranches in the Far West," *Fortnightly Review,* Vol. XXXIV (1880), 457. Abbott and Smith, *We Pointed Them North,* 162. Dick, *Vanguards of the Frontier,* 477–78. Haley, *The XIT Ranch of Texas,* 163. Abernathy, *In Camp With Theodore Roosevelt,* 37. Frank T. Mattison, *A History of the Episcopal Church in Northwest Texas,* 44.
[21] John Baumann, "On a Western Ranche," *Fortnightly Review,* Vol. XLVII (1887), 531.

The rise and fall of the range cattle industry is a story within itself, and involves considerably more than the coming of barbed wire and small farmers and overstocking the range. A true boom set in in 1880 and spiraled wildly until 1886, when the industry suffered a reverse from which it never recovered. In the meantime, cattle profits had been magnified into fantastic figures in eastern and non-American journals and by word of mouth, and were accepted all the more readily for being incredible. Men everywhere—in the United States, in England, in Scotland, and in Canada—poured in capital in a mad struggle for the control of public land for grazing purposes (sounds like 1946–1950, doesn't it?).

Overstocking was already being felt, as was wire fencing. Severe droughts hit Texas. But the crushing blow began to descend in November, 1886, when snow fell so deeply upon the plains that in places the cattle could not get through to the grass. The winter's grip held, and those cattlemen who hadn't laid by hay began to pray for a warming chinook to rescue them. In early January the warm winds did come, and hopes rose. But on January 30 the northwest was swept by a blizzard such as no plainsman could remember. The cattle wandered aimlessly looking for grazing that was buried beyond reach. Men were compelled to huddle in their ranch headquarters for weeks while the high, cold, bitter winds swept past. When at last spring arrived and the cattlemen went forth timorously to see the results, they found their cattle piled in coulees, or else wandering about emaciated, with frozen ears, tails, and feet, and on legs so weak they could barely stand.[22]

The winter of 1886–1887 was the sort of sharp punch calculated to puncture permanently an overblown specula-

[22] Osgood, *The Day of the Cattleman*, 220–21.

tive bubble. From that time forward, unreasoned speculations tended to be abandoned and a completely new, reasonably orderly approach was taken to the ranching industry. Ranching, like any other long-range industry, began to seek and find formulas for survival against all sorts of exigencies, and began also to take on some of the aspects of modern business procedure. It was better business but decidedly less picturesque.

By 1892, the story of the frontier ranch and its cowboys had already been lived, and many cowboys were getting ready to reminisce in print and at cowboy reunions. Already the cowboy had become a myth which would become more firmly imbedded in the folk mind with the passing of each year until truth and fiction were inextricable. Despite his short, but definite, life span, covering principally the years from 1867 to 1885, the American cowboy of the frontier trail driving days and the range and ranch frontier was on his way to becoming a timeless symbol for the frontier panorama of the Great Plains.

5. The Myth

"Ma," says she, "do cowboys eat grass?"
"No, dear," says the old lady, "they're part human."
CHARLES M. RUSSELL,
Trails Plowed Under.

SIXTY-FIVE years after the open range has all but disappeared, cowboys still herd cattle in the West, still ride horses, still hold roundups. And ranches, though fenced, still spread over ranges almost as extensive as the spreads of Goodnight and Littlefield and Iliff nearly three-quarters of a century ago. Less than a decade ago, there remained nearly a thousand ranches of more than 20,000 acres each: 262 of these—most of them in Texas, New

68

Mexico, and Arizona—contained upward of 100,000 acres.[1]

But the cowboy belongs to the past as surely as if his day had completely ended with the coming of fence and farmer. Those images arising whenever the word "cowboy" is mentioned—the man on horseback, armed with his six-shooter, trailing a thousand longhorns across virgin prairie, keeping a squinted eye out for Comanche, Apache, or Sioux, wondering whether the buffalo will survive another season before the onslaught of the hunters—those instantaneous images of the cowboy belong as definitely to the past as do, say, the Indian fighters of the days of Daniel Boone. The Great West still has spaciousness and aridity framed with mountains that beckon, but it is as surely civilized as New England, and Denver is as up-to-date a city as Hartford, and twice as large. There are differences between the United States, east and west, but the differences narrow perceptibly, and the Easterner making his first trip into the trans-Mississippi area is usually more struck by how undifferent Kansas is from New Jersey than he is by a feeling that now he is out with the frontiersman. For the frontier has faded, and the cowboy, although he is still around physically, faded with the frontier.

Actually there is a sort of timelessness in this consignment of the cowboy to the past, all the while he is galloping across the plains of our imaginations. The myth of the American cowboy arose before the trails closed, before the open range closed, while the frontier cowboy was still meeting the challenge of frontier conditions. Look at him as early as 1887, when one British traveler described him thus:

The cowboy has at the present time become a personage; nay, more, he is rapidly becoming a mythical one. Distance is doing for him what lapse of time did for the heroes of antiquity. His

[1] J. W. Williams, *The Big Ranch Country*, 260.

admirers are investing him with all manner of romantic qualities; they descant upon his manifold virtues and his pardonable weaknesses as if he were a demi-god, and I have no doubt that before long there will be ample material for any philosophic inquirer who may wish to enlighten the world as to the cause and meaning of the cowboy myth. Meanwhile, the true character of the cowboy has been obscured, his genuine qualities are lost in fantastic tales of impossible daring and skill, of daring equitations and unexampled endurance. Every member of his class is pictured as a kind of Buffalo Bill, as a long-haired ruffian who, decked out in gaudy colors, and tawdry ornaments, booted like a cavalier, chivalrous as a Paladin, his belt stuck full of knives and pistols, makes the world to resound with bluster and braggadocio.[2]

Among all the frontier children of the Old West, the cowboy proved the most irresistible, and it is this folk character that fiction writers have enshrined in more pages of print than any other figure in the history of Anglo-American folk life on this side of the Atlantic. Edward Everett Dale, the Oklahoma historian and raconteur, saw it this way:

So it is also true that you may enclose the green prairies and plow up the sweet wildflowers, you may build towns and cities on sites once occupied by the cowboy's dugout and branding pen, but always something of the fragance of the romance of the early days will cling to the region which the bold range riders once called their own, to remind us of those picturesque days gone forever.[3]

Curiously, the American cowboy never became personified and idealized in any one character, but has re-

[2] Baumann, "On a Western Ranche," *Fortnightly Review*, Vol. XLVII (1887), 516.
[3] "The Romance of the Range," *West Texas Historical Year Book*, Vol. V (June, 1929), 21.

mained a composite telescoped into a single folk type. Removing the miraculous from the deeds of Achilles and Beowulf, you must rank the cowboy alongside these traditional heroes in accomplishment. There is, however, no single cowboy to represent him, as Kit Carson personifies the mountain man or William F. Cody—"Buffalo Bill"—the buffalo hunter. Nor has he a synthetic and exaggerated representation, as Paul Bunyan belongs to the woods and lumber, and as John Henry belongs to the levee and the railroad. This lack exists in spite of the fact that the cowboy, for all his renowned reserve, was his own greatest press agent. In the frontier days, he kicked up enough dust in Kansas, and, dressed uniquely or outrageously, according to the viewer's taste, caused enough commotion on those sporadic forays into more settled centers like Chicago; and after the frontier days, realizing that his had been a different and a passing life, he rushed into print with enough memoirs of all sorts and hues to get his fame or notoriety broadcast to almost every country in the world. No second-echelon New Dealer ever wanted worse to tell what he had seen and heard and experienced.

While the cowboy was operating on the range, eastern visitors would pay for the privilege of watching him work. After he quit operating, they continued to pay, watching him, as enacted successively by such strong-visaged men as Bill Hart, Tom Mix, or Tex Ritter, or reading of his exploits, as seen through the red-streaked eyes of some studio fictioneer who picked up his squint under a fluorescent lamp.

From the outset, the range rider has embodied all of the virtues and vices of the Anglo-American in one folk type. You can accept him either as completely good or as completely bad, or as a Robin Hood who will bend the law to aid the unfortunate. Good or bad, he meets the challenges of the day, never quailing before odds, never craven when facing a stampede or the exit end of a Winchester's barrel.

Ideally the American cowboy was a superb horseman, which as a fact he was; an expert of the fast draw and the use of a Colt revolver, which he might have been; a dead shot with a Winchester; brave beyond question; always on the side of justice, even if that justice be a bit stern at times; the defender of virtuous women; the implacable foe of the Indian; and a man to whom honor and integrity came naturally. As such he has been depicted in fiction, and undoubtedly as such he really existed here and there, as good men exist everywhere in all ages.

On the other hand, the "bad man" tradition is just as strong and in addition has wrapped itself around some real people whose extraordinary, if not altogether admirable, exploits have survived the myth-making process as individuals. In one way or another, James Butler Hickok, Ben Thompson, John Wesley Hardin, Sam Bass, and William H. Bonney are associated with the cattleman's frontier. Ben Thompson ran a saloon in Abilene; "Wild Bill" Hickok was town marshal of Abilene until he was in effect fired for two cold-blooded murders; John Wesley Hardin visited Abilene as a trail driver. Sam Bass was a cowboy whose trail boss, Joel Collins, gambled away money he owed for a herd he had sold in Deadwood, Dakota. To recoup, so that he might repay his friends, Collins robbed a Union Pacific train of 60,000 dollars a few miles from Ogallala. Bass helped him. Here is Robin Hood in a coat of tarnished tin. Debts to one's friends must be paid—that is good; but to get the money, a robbery is staged—that is bad.

As no other individual in frontier days, Billy the Kid— William H. Bonney—a cowboy by occupation and a sometimes horse thief, cattle rustler, and man-killer by practice and circumstance, has come to symbolize the "bad man" in a considerable body of folklore which swells with each succeeding year. Fairly recently, Marshall Fishwick wrote that " 'The Saga of Billy the Kid' is required reading for the student of the heroic process in America." In many ways, he added, "William H. Bonney symbolized the whole pastoral epoch doomed by the railroad, tractor, and homesteader." [4]

Billy the Kid was an undersized youth who had indisputable courage, who had been wronged, who fought against odds, and who gave no quarter and asked none. He was probably psycopathic, but Americans didn't trouble themselves about that then. All they knew was that here was a nerveless man who fought hard and died hard, and they regarded him with a mixture of reverence and abhorrence; but they did regard him. It is not difficult to see what the publicity that surrounded Bonney, Bass, Hickok, and the others would do for the perpetuation and enlargement of the cowboy mythology.

The etymology of the term itself lends authority to the "bad man" connotation, though no romance or adventure was associated with the word till the trail drives began to Abilene. *Cowboy* showed up in the American Revolution in the neutral ground of Westchester County, New York, where the loyalist Cowboys and the more or less patriot Skinners intermittently raided and plundered each other, with cattle a principal object of theft. In fact, it was the Skinners who stopped Major John André and turned him and the Benedict Arnold papers over to the American authorities. But aside from that digression, a *cowboy* was not

[4] "Billy the Kid: Faust in America," *Saturday Review*, Vol. XXXV (October 11, 1952), 35–36. See also Pat Garrett, *The Authentic Life of Billy the Kid* (Norman, University of Oklahoma Press, 1954).

a person to be admired especially, for he was an armed Tory not above tinkling a cowbell to "beguile the patriots into the brush hunting for cows." [5]

Texas did little to improve the associations of *cowboy*. As has been already noted, following the Texas Revolution, constant friction went on between the Texans and the Mexicans, which particularly took the form of raids on each other's cattle. Leading the forays against the Mexicans were these Texas "cowboys," who were not above moving into a Mexican's property some moonlit night, rushing off his cattle for twenty-four hours or so, and then driving them leisurely to the Texas Gulf Coast or on to New Orleans. The odium attached to the Texas "cowboy" is clearly manifest in the words of one writer of the 1850's:

The old man was a cattle driver, or "cowboy," as those men are and were termed who drove in the cattle of the Mexican rancheros of the Rio Grande border, either by stealth, or after plundering or murdering the herdsman! They were, in short, considered as banditti before the Revolution, and have been properly considered so since. This term, "cowboy," was even then—and still more emphatically later—one name for many crimes; since those engaged in it were mostly outlaws confessedly, and if not so at the beginning, were driven into outlawry by the harsh and stern contingencies of their pursuit, which, as it was in violation of all law, compelled them frequently into the most heinous crimes, to protect themselves from entailed consequences. [6]

That the Texas "cowboy" would have risen above his early unsavory reputation if longhorn cattle raising had remained a purely Texas institution is unlikely, in which

[5] William A. Craigie and James R. Hurlburt (eds.), *A Dictionary of American English*, II, 658. Carl Van Doren, *Secret History of the American Revolution*, 339-40.

[6] Charles W. Webber, *Tales of the Southern Border*, 124. Dobie, *A Vaquero*, 46, 59-61.

case he probably would never have left such an indelible stamp on American folk life. But when a later generation who were not border ruffians at all but usually semi-Southern cavaliers with a cattle stamp came working northward, then the cowboy as we know him emerged from the woods of opprobrium and came to stay in the hearts of his fellow Americans, both contemporary and future. Thereafter it was recognized that there were bad men among the cowboys, but to brand the class as bad would have been as unfair as damning farmers as a class because some unprincipled son-of-Cincinnatus actively coveted his neighbor's wife, cattle, or outbuildings.

Undoubtedly the ever-present six-gun played a role in painting the cowboy as a lawless frontiersman. The occasional cowboy on a spree, tasting what McCoy calls "this vortex of dissipation," dancing with drunken abandon with that sad Victorian creature, "the soiled dove," dressed in sombrero, spurs, and pistol still, might easily frighten the uninitiated.[7] It was as natural as dust that he should shout like a demon—hadn't the Rebels yelled?—and when hilarity reached its peak, even discharge his pistol a time or two to provide exclamation marks to the evening's rowdiness. To people who don't normally associate with guns, be they holed up fearfully within hearing distance in their Abilene homes or within reading distance in Fall River, Massachusetts, such behavior smacks of an inherent lawlessness. Follow that with the reckless ride through the town's streets, with pistol blazing merrily at nothing in particular, or with the quarrel and the quick draw outside the Red Light saloon, and the trip afterward to Boot Hill, and multiply the experience by Wichita, Newton, Ellsworth, and Dodge City, which for ten years held forth as the greatest cattle trading mart in the world, and you have

[7] McCoy, *Historic Sketches*, 209.

more than adequate reason to support your belief that the cowboy is an incorrigible outlaw. They are, said one foreign observer in the 1880's, "the plague of the West . . . too idle to work in the mines or on the farms . . . invariably . . . drunk and . . . a terror to the inhabitants." [8]

Not all the violence in the Kansas cowtowns was the fault of the cowboy, although he was the most conspicuous participant. Money turning over entices people to assist in the turnover, regardless of principle. So people came to Kansas to share in and to augment the "toil, trouble, boil and bubble" of booming, unsettled communities—both exploiting sexes, greedy, merciless, soulless, birds of prey and birds of a dubious paradise, seeking the dollar by whatever device and deceit. It's the story of boom towns in all ages in all places—Old Tascosa and Mobeetie in Texas, for cowboys; Virginia City, Nevada or Montana, for miners; Pithole City, Pennsylvania, for nineteenth century oil prospectors, and Ranger and Kilgore, Texas, for twentieth century oilmen; the Klondike, for gold miners; and now Utah, for uranium seekers.

Tinseled temptation then abounded, and cowboys, especially the younger, less wary ones, were human beings fresh in from a long, lonely, tiring journey with payday in their pockets. Many of them succumbed, and some of them got out of hand. But, as George W. Saunders, an old-time trail driver wrote, "it is not fair to besmear the name of the cowboy with the deeds of every outlaw in the country. I know the majority of these cowboys made the best citizens in Texas." [9] Theodore Roosevelt, who had a mildly astringent view toward the West, opined that the Easterner tended to call a cowboy every person wearing a broad hat

[8] E. de Mandet-Graney, *Cow-boys and Colonels*, 27.
[9] Hunter, *The Trail Drivers of Texas*, 966.

and carrying a six-gun,[10] while Robert M. Wright, mayor of Dodge City during a part of its bovine heyday, paid the cowboy the following compliment:

The genuine Texas cowboy is worth describing. In many respects he is a wonderful creature. He endures many hardships that would take the lives of most men, and is therefore a perfect specimen of physical manhood. He is the finest horseman. . . . He aims to be a dead shot . . . there are less cut-throats and murderers graduated from the cowboy than from the better class who come from the east for venture of gain. They delight in appearing rougher than they are. [11]

The Texas cowboy then strapped on his six-gun and went to Kansas. At home he wouldn't have left off his Colt because he could need it for anything from Indians to charging wild cattle. At the end of the trail, he wore it in a holster attached to his belt as naturally as today's businessman straps a tie around his neck. But Kansans didn't wear guns that way, and the ever-present revolver excited their imaginations, and they enlarged the myth of the Texas cowboy till it seemed he settled every argument, no matter how trifling, with gunplay. E. C. Abbott, drawing on his own cowboy experience, perhaps gives the lie to this exaggeration as effectively as any other source when he writes as follows:

I would like to say more about this business of gun fights, because so much has been made about it in fiction, and it is nearly all exaggeration as far as this part of this country is concerned. I worked up here from 1883 on and I saw a lot of hard work on the range but very little shooting. In fact, from '85 on, until it quit being a range, there never was but one shooting

[10] Roosevelt, *Ranch Life and the Hunting Trail*, 19.
[11] *Dodge City, Cowboy Capital*, 282–83.

scrape in Maginni district, and then nobody got killed; and over on the Judith and the Mocassin, which were the next ranges, they never had one.[12]

The Colt revolver did play an important role in subduing the Great Plains frontier, a role much more important than these statements would suggest, but in a manner dissociated from general hellishness. As far as the range rider is concerned, the six-shooter has been credited with use entirely disproportionate with the facts.

Adding as much to the myth of the cowboy as his six-gun has been the range rider's colorful dress, which in the middle twentieth century is as likely to be seen on a six-year-old of either sex astride a stick horse in Greenwich, Connecticut, as on a bona fide Colorado cowman. The wide-brimmed sombrero, the high-heeled boots, the bright neckpiece, usually a bandana—these were, and are, distinguishing features of a man of the range, or of a man who wishes he were. Although it is usually referred to as a sombrero, actually the cowboy's hat as likely derived from the Southern cavalry hat as from below the Rio Grande. The sun beats down, not simply shines, in Texas for months on end. A man's hat may be his only shade, so give him enough brim for him to take cover under and enough crown to stay on no matter how blue and ornery the norther he may have to head into later.

The high-heeled boots, which national magazines persist in showing Texas college students wearing with tuxedos, a practice indulged in only when photographers are handy, are timelessly identified with the range riders and are often dismissed by the Easterner as a Western conceit. Actually, like the broad-brimmed hat, the high-heeled boot makes sense, as the Asiatic plainsman of a thousand years

[12] Abbott and Smith, *We Pointed Them North*, 250.

ago could have told you. He used them, as did and does the cowboy, to keep his foot secure in the stirrup. In 1850, just before the cowboy era, a gentleman's riding boot had the same high heel which turned up in Abilene a decade and a half later.[13] Besides, no footwear combines utility and comfort more than the Western cowboy boot, not to mention its further contribution to the rolling gait with which the cowboy saunters when aground. Not even a scion of the Atlantic Coast who never saw a horse outside Central Park bridle paths can escape walking like an ol' cowhand in a pair of Western cowboy boots!

E. C. Abbott recalled with candor if not altogether with accuracy that the old-time cowboys wore wide-brimmed beaver hats, black or brown, with low crowns, fancy shirts, high-heeled boots, and not infrequently vests, usually unbuttoned to prevent sweating. All cowboys had a pair of bullhide leggings, or chaps. Both clothes and saddles were locally made. Most cowboys had an army coat with cape which served as blanket and slicker. As time passed, according to Abbott, the low-crowned beaver yielded to the high, white-crowned Stetson, and fancy shirts and pants came to be store bought. On the northern plains, the range riders wore good cloth overcoats with beaver collars and cuffs. To complete the uniform, there were the Colt revolver, originally with a foot-long barrel later cut down to six or seven and a half inches and a black rubber, pearl, or ivory handle, and spurs, at first with big belled rowels which in time gave way to hand-forged silver inlaid spurs with droop shanks and small rowels.[14]

The description which Granville Stuart gives would still be largely unchanged:

[13] R. Turner Wilcox, *The Mode in Footwear*, 142. Emerson Hough, *The Story of the Cowboy*, 52–53.

[14] Abbott and Smith, *We Pointed Them North*, 9.

They wore the best clothes they could buy and took great pride in their personal appearance and in their trapping. The men of our outfit used to pay $25.00 a pair for made-to-order riding boots when the best store boots in Helena were $10.00 a pair. Their trappings consisted of a fine saddle, silver mounted bridle, pearl-handled six-shooter, latest model cartridge belt with silver buckle, silver spurs, a fancy quirt with silver mountings, a fine riata sometimes made of rawhide, a pair of leather chaps, and a fancy hatband often made from the dressed skin of a diamond rattlesnake. They wore expensive stiff-brimmed light felt hats with brilliantly colored handkerchief knotted about their necks, light colored shirts and exquisitely fitted high-heeled riding boots.[15]

Gaily, gaudily bedecked, this figure rode the range. Isolated by time and distance, two necessary elements for any myth, he should have been far removed from the public eye, but somehow he hit a responsive chord in the American fancy until he, the cowboy, just one of several types of Westerners, became the typical Westerner. As one writer observed, "For every hired man on horseback there have been hundreds of plowmen in America, and tens of millions of acres of rangelands plowed under, but who can cite a single autobiography of a laborer in the fields of cotton, of corn, or wheat?"[16] There was, wrote Walter Prescott Webb,

. . . something romantic about him. He lives on horseback as do the Bedouins; he fights on horseback, as did the knights of chivalry; he goes armed with a strange new weapon which he uses ambidextrously and precisely; he swears like a trooper, drinks like a fish, wears clothes like an actor, and fights like a devil. He is gracious to ladies, reserved toward strangers, gen-

[15] *Forty Years*, II, 183.
[16] Dobie, *Guide to Life and Literature of the Southwest*, 90.

erous to his friends, and brutal to his enemies. He is a cowboy, a typical Westerner.[17]

At least seventy years ago, the contention was made that this American cowboy was one of our national folk heroes, an integral part of our social culture, a broad mythological archetype, though the contention was phrased more simply. Since then, other writers have repeated the assertion. He may have claimed to be "merely folks, just plain, everyday, bowlegged humans," but his public will have none of that. As time has passed, the partisans of the cowboy myth have multiplied to include historians, fiction writers, ballad composers, folk singers, artists, and of course the cowboy himself.[18] Working independently but proceeding together, these groups have continuously publicized the cowboy, and at the same time have helped to crystallize the myth. Unabashedly sentimental, especially the cowhand recollector, they vacillate between the lyrical and the mystical as they recreate the cattleman's empire. Occasionally the old cowman at the annual reunion will come back to reality long enough to deny that he ever shone in armor or indeed did anything more than eat dust on horseback because it was his job and he had no choice but to endure its demands and discomforts. But his lapse into reality is strictly temporary, and he soon rejoins his narrating brethren to spread the word of cowboys who were more gods than men, of horses that by comparison would make Pegasus limp with four clubbed feet, and of mossy-horned cattle that could surpass the combined cerebrations of the Institute of Advanced Learning. The desire to deify the cowboy seems

[17] *The Great Plains*, 496.
[18] Mody C. Boatright, "The American Myth Rides the Range," *Southwest Review*, Vol. XXXVI, No. 3 (Summer, 1951), 158. Philip Ashton Rollins, *The Cowboy*, 40.

to infect even the most normally disenchanted observer.

As yet, there has been no real philosophical probing into why this penchant for mysticism should prevail nor why there should be a cowboy myth in American folk life at all. As we make no pretensions at being philosophers, you won't find the answer here. You won't find it anywhere else either. But there is no denying that the cowboy myth does exist, that it is fundamental to an understanding of the cultural content of American life, nor that it is real.

6. The Lawless

THE legends which have accumulated about the "Lawless West" have a sounder historical foundation than many Americans suppose. Americans may like to talk about the Westerner's being a chronic law violator, but they tend to think of this talk as so much more exaggeration in a land that is not noted for its modesty. But the claim that the West was lawless at certain places and at certain times on the frontier is a fact, as Walter Prescott Webb explains in his *Great Plains:*

The West was lawless for two reasons: first, because of the social conditions that obtained there during the period under consideration; secondly, because the law that was applied there was not made for the conditions that existed and was unsuitable for those conditions. It did not fit the needs of the country, and could not be obeyed.[1]

In that early period on the frontier, the restraint of law and order could not be exercised. The vast distances that had to be traversed between populated centers on the Great Plains and the absolute readiness with which the Westerner could move from one place to another made it an easy matter for him deliberately to become lost to an officer to the law. Under such conditions, each man had to make and enforce his own law, for there was no one else to do it for him. A man's survival depended upon his physical strength, his personal courage, and his ability to use fire arms. Since he moved among armed men, he was sometimes compelled to resort to the use of the six-shooter for survival.[2]

Small wonder then that, as the railroad and telegraph with their quick communication with the more routine East pushed westward into the cattleman's country and as the word spread that a cowboy and his six-shooter were inseparable, the cowboy came to be thought of as a man with a gun, a man who, in the words of Webb, "wears it low and pulls it smokin'," [3] who dominated the entire West "with a horse and a six-shooter in the interest of cattle." [4]

When you speak of six-shooter or revolver, you mean in this instance the invention of Samuel Colt, who took out his first patent at the time the Texas revolution was getting underway. How the six-gun found its way to Texas is uncertain, but apparently it had made the trip by the

[1] *The Great Plains,* 496.
[2] *Ibid.,* 496–97.
[3] "The American Revolver and the West," *Scribner's Magazine,* Vol. LXXXI (January–June, 1927), 171.
[4] *Ibid.,* 178.

end of the 1830's, where it was promptly utilized to fight the Indians, who with their lances and arrows till then could rush the Texas between reloadings of their single-shot muskets and pistols. By 1853, the Colt had made sufficient progress in Texas to impress at least Charles W. Webber as he wrote his story, "Pinto Trace":

We were about fourteen men to eighty stout and well-armed warriors. We routed them from their chosen position on the hill, and with the loss of three men and four wounded, literally cut them to pieces—killing nearly half their whole number. But for our revolvers, the attack would never have been made; and had it been, we should only have been awfully whipped.[5]

Fiction writers are especially fond of strapping two Colts on their heroes, a device which is all right if the timing is correct. The earlier Colts were cap-and-ball affairs of somewhat erratic quality, so that a second afforded some protection in case the first failed, plus the fact that the cap-and-ball was slow to reload. But with improvements in the Colt and the introduction of the metallic cartridge, the need for the second gun was diminished and one was usually the rule, though it was one rule that Wild Bill Hickok, for instance, never observed. One student of cowboy ways gives this description of the cowboy and his guns:

When one recalls [writes Philip Ashton Rollins] that the gun actually carried . . . was the forty-five or forty-four caliber, eight-inch barrelled, single-action Colt's revolver, weighing two and a quarter pounds, and that its ammunition weighed something in addition; when one recalls also that the average cowpuncher was not an incipient murderer, but was only an average man and correspondingly lazy, then one realizes to be

[5] *Tales,* 302.

true the statements that the average puncher was unwilling to encumber himself with more than one gun, and often even failed to "go heeled". . . to the extent of "packing". . . . unless conditions insistently demanded. These insistent conditions were, first, expectation of attack by a personal enemy; second, service near the Mexican border or in an Indian-infested country; third, a ride on the Range where there might be met human trespassers, or be encountered either animals dangerous to stock or stock hopelessly injured or diseased . . . ; fourth . . . either a holiday visit to another ranch or to town, or else a formal call on a girl.

The gun not only was an integral part of full dress, but also was to the mind of the cowboy as effective on the female heart, and as compelling an accompaniment of love-making as to the belief of the young soldier has ever been the sword.[6]

Generally speaking, the cowboy's accuracy with his six-shooter is vastly overrated, largely because the Colt wasn't likely to hit where it was aimed beyond a range of twenty-five to thirty yards. In fact, the old cap-and-ball revolver couldn't equal either the range or deadliness of the Indian bow and arrow, though the later Colt of 1870 and after, with its improved range and metallic cartridge, equalized the contest between Indian and white man. The more deadly weapon was the Winchester, which, though widely used, lacked the all-round utility and handiness of the six-shooter. Once the buffalo and Indian had moved from the scene and the range cattleman had yielded to the nester and the wire fence, the day of the six-gun was over and, in the words of one writer, "became even an object of obnoxious legislation."[7]

[6] Rollins, *The Cowboy*, 41.
[7] Chauncey Thomas, "Frontier Firearms," *Colorado Magazine*, Vol. VII, No. 3 (May, 1930), 103–106. To cite two evidences of the high standing of the Winchester, Buffalo Bill Cody wrote the Winchester Company in 1875 that he considered the latest model *"the boss. . . .*

A frequent incident in Western fiction is the six-gun duel involving the town marshal, Texas Ranger, desperado, or cowboy, each with two guns and equally proficient with either. This myth has some historical foundation, as there were men who were consummate artists with their six-shooters and who hated other men with a sufficient passion to shoot it out in public, though probably more men were ambushed or shot in the back than ever shot it out in a saloon. This is a belief, rather than a statement of fact, as statistics weren't kept on this sort of thing.

The typical six-gun duel begins in a saloon as the swinging door opens wide to admit one of the protagonists, who promptly spots the other. There follows the lightning draw as both men blaze away murderously at each other until one or both are down, preferably permanently. If you haven't read such a story or seen it on the movie screen, it's your own fault, for such a scene is a capital fixture in the Western myth. It is familiar and, in the hands of a good narrator or director, quite effective.

Such a gun battle occurred in Arizona between Pete Gabriel, sheriff at Globe, and Joe Phy, a former assistant dismissed for brutal abuse of a prisoner. Phy no longer liked Gabriel; in fact, his hatred obsessed him, and he took every opportunity to try to goad Gabriel into drawing on him. Phy, who was reputed to be the better shot, ambidextrous and tremendously skillful, practiced by the hour, and Globe waited—a fiction writer would say, "with bated breath."

In May, 1888, Gabriel was drinking with his friends,

An Indian will give more for one of your rifles than any other gun he can get"; while in Idaho in 1888–1889, some town founders suggested that the projected town be named for whichever gun was carried by the most people present, with the result that Winchester, Idaho, came into being. Harold F. Williamson, *Winchester, The Gun That Won the West,* 67, 102.

when, in the best scenario style, Phy kicked open the swinging door, revolver in one hand, Bowie knife in the other, and started shooting. The first shot struck Gabriel just below the heart, piercing the lung. Gabriel, with instantaneous reflexes, shot Phy in the pit of the stomach and then advanced on him, firing as he neared. Gabriel was hit three more times, in the side, wrist, and body. One of the shots put out the lights, after which the shooting went on in semidarkness. As Gabriel reached the door to grab for his opponent, Phy fell through the swinging doors and pitched on the sidewalk. By two o'clock in the morning, Phy was dead, while Gabriel began a slow recovery.[8] No script writer ever conceived it better—or bloodier.

The foregoing encounter points up two facts. For one thing, the firing was all at short range, as proper six-gun shooting should be to be on target. Further, neither man was cowboy, though in all likelihood the same story transferred to fiction would place Phy in a cowboy's chaps, his cowboy hat aslant at a perilous angle. The average cowboy was not a gunman, nor had he a notch in his gun. His occupation was tending cattle. Carousing was widely spaced, and fighting was relatively seldom. Forty thousand cowboys spread out over the Great Plains. Forty thousand people anywhere will produce some troublemakers, even at a protracted revival; and the cowboy, isolated a good part of the year from outside companionship and convivialities, produced at least his share of both one-shot and habitual hellhounds. But as a class, he does not deserve the lawless tag.

But there is a badman tradition in the story of the cowboy, and because it persists and because it is not without basis, it deserves a look. The tradition hails from Kansas

[8] Con P. Cronin, "Arizona's Six-Gun Classic," *Arizona Historical Review*, Vol. III, No. 2 (July, 1930), 8–10.

and strings westward as the cattle depots followed the extension of the railroad and the line of settlement toward the mountains. As has been already noted, Abilene was first in the sequence, and enough has been said of that cowtown already to indicate that it was somewhat less than genteel. Texas Street, with its saloons, its dance halls, gaming room, women—and in a class not noted for high principle, Abilene women rated especially low, as so many of them had come west because they were too rough for St. Louis or Kansas City, and among the courtesans, which is certainly a euphemism if ever there was one, were more than one who had killed a man the quick way—all provided a setting in which a slightly befuddled man could get off on the wrong foot with his morals and with the law.[9] Quickly Abilene became so notorious that it almost attained the respectability of fame, and staid Easterners, including the wealthy, the noted, and the plain curious, took trains to Abilene just to see whether the tales they heard were true. One look at the town marshal, Wild Bill Hickok, with his flowing mane and his two ivory-handled pistols protruding ostentatiously was usually sufficient to send them home convinced.

Hickok was not the first Abilene marshal. The first several failed quickly. Then in May, 1870, Abilene named Thomas J. Smith to that post, and he deserves considerable credit as the man who settled Abilene down. He ordered a ban on firearms within the town limits, working on the theory that liquor and guns don't make good companions. Hardly had he been given his badge of authority when on Saturday "Big Hank," a cowboy with more than his share of obnoxious behavior, approached Smith, boasting that no one could disarm him. When Smith demanded the gun, Big Hank swore back at him, at which Smith promptly

[9] Henry, *Conquering Our Great American Plains*, 120.

felled the cowboy with his fists. On Sunday, an almost identical episode took place between Smith and another cowboy. After that, Smith had little trouble, most of the Texas cowboys became his loyal supporters, and guns disappeared from the streets of Abilene. Unfortunately, in November, Smith went with a party to arrest a homesteader outside Abilene for murder, only to wind up murdered himself.[10]

The following April, 1871, Abilene employed a new town marshal named James B. Hickok. The salary was 150 dollars a month plus 25 per cent of all fines from arrests made by him.[11] The man was mean, but he was memorable. Six feet tall, 175 pounds, sinuous, graceful, cool, long wavy brown hair worn shoulder-length, flowing moustache, delicate hands, almost feminine feet, low-voiced, impeccably dressed, nerveless—such a man hadn't been seen since the Mississippi River gambler had faded from the scene. Governor Otero of New Mexico called him "beyond a shadow of a doubt . . . the most fearless, and perhaps the most dangerous man . . . on the frontier."[12]

Hickok's law enforcement in the summer of 1871 caused considerable discussion and not a little criticism. Most of his time he spent in the Alamo saloon while his assistants attended to the routine. However, despite the addition of several special officers, they were unable to cope with the tremendous influx of Texans during the cattle season. Toward the end of the season, Hickok and several Texans, encouraged by Phil Coe and Ben Thompson, proprietors of

[10] T. C. Henry, quoted in "Two City Marshals," *Transactions of the Kansas State Historical Society*, Vol. IX (1905–1906), 529–31.
[11] George L. Cushman, "Abilene, First of the Kansas Cowtowns," *The Kansas Historical Quarterly*, Vol. IX, No. 3 (August, 1940), 252–53.
[12] Miguel Antonio Otero, *My Life on the Frontier, 1864–1882*, 14–15.

the Bull's Head saloon, began an open feud. About nine o'clock on October 5, Hickok was in the Alamo when he heard a shot outside. Hickok hurried through the open door—always through the door!—and demanded who had fired.

Phil Coe, "a red-mouthed, bawling thug," pistol in hand in violation of the local ordinance, replied that he had shot at a dog, though no dog was in sight. Without hesitation, from eight feet away Wild Bill promptly shot Coe fatally, growling slightly because his usually impeccable aim was a bit low in the abdomen. The marshal himself received a hole in his coat and a breeze between his legs from a second shot.

A deputy, Mike Williams, hearing the shots, rushed to the scene. Hickok, not recognizing him, shot again, and Williams was dead. Five minutes later there wasn't a Texas cowboy in town. The Texans, as well as the town citizens, except for maybe a few of Wild Bill's mistresses scattered about the environs, felt the marshal was a mad dog, but as it was near the end of the season, it seemed the easier way to permit Hickok to serve out his contract. He was not re-hired, as it was generally agreed that his marksmanship was far superior to his character.[13]

Abilene had enough of cowboys and gun-toting marshals. Notice was sent to Texas during the winter that Texas cattle need no longer point their bellowing way toward Abilene. Eighty per cent of the citizens of Dickinson County signed the petition:

[13] Cushman, "Abilene, First of the Kansas Cowtowns," *The Kansas Historical Quarterly*, Vol. IX, No. 3 (August, 1940), 256. Henry, *Conquering Our Great American Plains*, 282. Gard, *The Chisholm Trail*, 173–79. Good examples of inaccurate mythmakers are Governor Otero, Lew Wallace, another New Mexico governor, and the lesser known M. J. Donoho, who in his hard-to-find *Circle-Dot* gets the time, the place, the participants, and the results generally wrong (168–170).

We, the undersigned members of the Farmer's Protective Association, and officers and citizens of Dickinson County, Kansas, most respectfully request all who have contemplated driving Texas cattle to Abilene the coming season to seek some other point for shipment, as the inhabitants of Dickinson will no longer submit to the evils of the trade.[14]

The Abilene story was repeated in little jumps all the way westward across Kansas and reads like a railway time-table. Ellsworth, "a tough little hole," took Abilene's place in 1872.[15] The next summer it added its bit to the legend in a battle similar to the Hickok-Coe affray, when Ben Thompson, of Texas, and John Sterling started quarreling over the division of their monte winnings. Sterling slapped Thompson, and before it was over the Ellsworth sheriff was dead. Sterling and Thompson, it might be added, were still going strong.[16]

Newton had its day. So did Hays City, which was further enlivened by the presence of "Calamity Jane"— the coarse Martha Jane Canary, who boasted she never went to bed sober. But the real rival to Abilene was the last of the Kansas cowtowns, Dodge City, "Queen of Cowtowns," "The Beautiful, Bibulous Babylon of the Frontier," or any of a half-dozen other titles that you might wish to apply. The Atchison, Topeka, and Santa Fe reached Dodge City in September, 1872. Ninety-five miles to the eastward was Hays City, the nearest point of legal justice. For Dodge, though, expeditious justice was much more easily attained on the spot, with the rifle or six-shooter balancing the scales of decision. The first jail was a well fifteen feet deep, which wasn't at all hard to guard. In the first year,

[14] Cushman, "Abilene, First of the Kansas Cowtowns," *The Kansas Historical Quarterly*, Vol. IX, No. 3 (August, 1940), 257.

[15] Otero, *My Life on the Frontier, 1864–1882*, 9.

[16] Floyd Benjamin Streeter, *Prairie Trails and Cowtowns*, 117–20. Gard, *The Chisholm Trail*, 201–203.

twenty-five men guilty of momentary bad judgment died with their boots on—gamblers, toughs, desperadoes, and one cowboy, to keep the myth alive.[17] "West of Kansas City," a movie advertisement was to claim sixty years later, "there was no law; West of Dodge City there was no God." Neither claim was correct, but it seemed almost credible at the time.

Dodge City soon proved to be a town the cowboys couldn't take over and run to suit themselves, for there were men present tougher than they. Here frontiersmen, hunters, and teamsters vied with the cowboy. Dodge City was a depot for three army posts and for a freighting service extending into all the surrounding country. When the railroads wanted fighters to protect their interests, they could find their hired gunmen in Dodge City. The combination of gunmen, bullwhackers, and determined citizenry represented more opposition than the cowboy cared to buck.

From 1875 to 1885, Dodge City billed itself as the "cowboy capital of the world," but in the latter year the quarantine law against Texas cattle turned away the last trail herd, and Kansas settled down to become a land of farmers. Dodge City was the last of the Kansas cowtowns, and as such, it was the last of the cowtowns anywhere, for the truly authentic cowtown belonged along that ragged line stretching across the Jayhawk state. Every Western territory and state had its cowtowns, but they were way stations adjacent to the range or the trail. The Kansas towns were the host towns, the towns at the end of the trail, the towns the cowboy had to visit before he could feel really accepted.

As these cowtowns were located in Kansas, some of the blood and fury spent by the cowboy in them was prob-

[17] Wright, *Dodge City,* 10, 141, 144, 171.

The Lawless 93

ably inevitable, because it must be remembered that the cowboy was primarily a Southern lad, and the war was a fresh, if not a personal, memory. Kansans were Yankees, northern gentlemen. The war was over, but what self-respecting cowboy could accept arrest meekly at the hands of a northern marshal? One Texas Ranger could arrest a dozen cowboys without incident; pride demanded maximum resistance if a northern sheriff came after you, and the cemeteries provided silent affirmation that too many Texans had unreasoning pride.

Without trying to be shrilly insistent, we have been at some pains to point out that forty thousand cowboys came north and that, considering the conditions, there were no larger percentage of cowboys who went wrong than there would be in any group of forty thousand. But with that point before us, we must still admit that the most infamous of the Western badmen was not a freighter, not a buffalo hunter, not a miner, but a cowboy. More of a thief, killer, and gambler, but a sometime cowboy nonetheless.

Billy the Kid was a product of a range war, a discussion of which will be deferred until the next chapter. But because Billy the Kid represents the accepted idea of a badman, and because he was a cowboy of sorts, he needs to be looked at in a little detail here.

Billy the Kid was a "kid," and a pint-sized one at that, but with "Colonel Colt's Equalizer" physical size in a man meant nothing. Westerners like to point out that he was born in New York's Bowery, but there is no denying he grew to manhood in Kansas, Colorado, and New Mexico. In the Lincoln County War of 1876–1878, he became the principal actor as he sought to avenge the murder of his onetime benefactor, an Englishman named J. H. Tunstall. He soon graduated from revenge to wholesale murder. By the time the war was over, Billy the Kid was said to have killed twenty-one men—one for each of his years on this earth, eight of them in the Lincoln County feud.[18] This estimate is probably a gross exaggeration. However, Governor Lew Wallace called him in for an interview and offered him safe conduct from New Mexico, but the Kid replied that this was his country and he was staying. Finally a former buffalo hunter and sometime drinking and monte pal of the Kid, giant Pat Garrett, started stalking him, and, in an encounter which the movies wouldn't permit, killed the Kid.

Garrett caught the Kid at Fort Sumner, where he had gone to be comforted by his *querida*. The tall sheriff let himself into the house of Pete Maxwell, thinking Maxwell might be able to tell him something of the Kid's whereabouts. It was one of those chance meetings. The Kid was at Maxwell's in another room. Sensing the presence of a stranger in the dark house, the Kid came quietly into Maxwell's bedroom, where Garrett sat at the edge of the bed. "*Quién es?*" the Kid called softly to the shadowy shape, marking one of the rare times in the presence of danger that he ever spoke first and shot later. Garrett fired twice at the direction from which the sound came, and that was all.[19] In the movies, and for that matter, in fiction, the two

[18] These statistics represent merely a fascination with matching numbers. The estimates of Billy the Kid's age and murders run up to 27. Ramon Adams, who is not distracted by legendary distortions, doubts that the Kid killed ten men, while J. C. Dykes, who has made an exhaustive search after the Kid, says the number should lie between a certain three and a probable six or seven. Even a scant three to ten, we might say, is above the national average! Ramon F. Adams (comp.), *Six-Guns & Saddle Leather*, 9. Pat F. Garrett, *The Authentic Life of Billy, the Kid*, xxiii–xxiv. J. C. Dykes, *Billy the Kid; The Bibliography of a Legend*, 6.

[19] Otero, *The Real Billy the Kid*, 27–43. Paul I. Wellman, *Glory, God and Gold: A Narrative History*, 368–75. Dobie, "Billy the Kid," *Southwest Review*, Vol. XIV, No. 3 (Spring, 1929), 316. George W. Coe, *Frontier Fighter*, 146–62.

would have sidled along down the main street, ducking behind buildings and under wagons, but always definitely aware of who and where the other was. Garrett would have given Billy the Kid, killer though he was, at least an opportunity to draw. In real life, Garrett preferred surprise and the sneak attack, which in a land of survival certainly makes more sense—and for a longer life.

Billy the Kid may furnish an extreme example of a fourth-rate cowboy becoming a first-rate killer, but it didn't take many such examples for the average observer from east of the Mississippi to decide that the naturally "Wild West" was in truth the "Lawless West." In Texas, following the Civil War, jobs for wages were scarce, and the cattle industry offered at least a job of sorts, plus the fact that if you were hiding, there were few more effective places to get lost than with a herd somewhere in the middle of millions of acres of Uncle Sam's grassland; so that some desperate men sought temporary refuge as cowboys. But most desperate men preferred the fiddle or the gaming table in town to the lonely harmonica in a bunkhouse two hundred hard miles from nowhere. What's the point of robbing a stagecoach if all you can spend it on is a new saddle and lariat?

A basic ingredient of the average movie or fiction story is the classic, brutal fist fight which occurs somewhere along the narrative way as a prelude to the eternal dispatching of the enemy cowboy or as the beginning of a beautiful and everlasting friendship. About fisticuffs, one thing can be said with certainty: the cowboy may have been nervous with a trigger or quick with a knife which, according to one inscription, he was never to "draw . . . without cause, nor sheathe . . . without honor," but he did not fight with his fists—either in a crowded barroom or teetering on the edge of a sheer canyon—not if there were a gun or a knife handy.[20] The cowboy had courage with a six-gun, or in the face of one, and the law of the West permitted a gun in protecting one's life, but fighting with fists on foot was demeaning and not for white men. Of course, he fought now and then. Sam Houston—not from Texas in those days—caned Congressman William Stanbery; in later days John L. Lewis pummeled his laboring colleague, Carpenter William Hutcheson, in full view of an American Federation of Labor convention, but neither these two incidents nor any sporadic outbreak in a banker's board meeting means that fighting is a basic ingredient of these men's lives or of their occupations. The truth is, the cowboy was not trained to use his fists, was as a class no good with them, and consequently was not disposed to take on any opponent unless his revolver or knife were handy. Fortunately, or unfortunately, they nearly always were. The magnificent fist fight which leaves the saloon divested, the onlookers exhausted, and the participants bloodstained is almost strictly a product of twentieth-century imagination.

To lift the cowboy, however, from his association with Western lawlessness adds nothing to his mythical stature. The average cowboy may never have hanged summarily —how else can you hang?—a horse thief, or slugged it out in a saloon, or rescued an abducted maiden—the beautiful and lovely, but altogether fictional cowgirl had not been invented in those days, but that is another story. He may have been merely a unique occupational type who was concerned with "cow work" on the range, raising, rounding up, branding, trailing, haying, and mending. But the American folk mind likes to enshrine him as a creature beyond and above the law, a cavalier, or *caballero*, who rode with the gods and who rode like a devil, a man who

[20] Cook, *Fifty Years on the Frontier*, 12–13.

carried his own rules loaded in his holster, and a man who enforced those rules according to his interpretation—a mounted prosecuting attorney, judge, jury, and executioner who dispatched all cases on the spot. He may not have been lawless, but the American imagination will keep him that way, you may be sure.

7. The Range Wars

THE range wars which the Westerners fought on the Great Plains over water and grazing rights of the public domain and over property rights in cattle, horses, sheep, and land have fascinated historical investigators, fiction writers, and movie makers alike. Unlike the drifters who passed through the individual rogues galleries of the lawless West, the men who participated in the range wars were the backbone of the frontier and the fathers of the settlement of the West. Their clashes were not based on pure deviltry or exuberant high jinks or parasitical greed, but were deadly serious encounters brought on by that most sacred nineteenth-century motivation, the protection of private property, as well as the preservation of a way of life. In a conflict between cattleman and rustler, or between enraged vigilantes and erring cowboy, the issue of right versus wrong might be clear-cut. But in the still bitterer conflict between cattleman and nester, or cattleman and sheepman, both sides might be right. Add to this battle, with its white and black nuances fusing into grey, the fact that so often the conflict also took on the aspect of the "littles" versus the "bigs" and you have the ingredients for anything from a morality play to a psychiatric study to a foreshadowing of Henry Wallace's common man jousting against the vested interests. Writers have approached the range wars on all these levels.

A basic difference between writing and literature is imagination. But imagination has added little to the historical facts which support the myths and legends of the range-war phase of the cattleman's frontier. With activities that justify dragging out the old saw about "stranger than fiction," the range wars seem to have overwhelmed the literary practitioners who have plumbed for psychological impulses or to have dissuaded the literary action-weavers from attempting any pattern more strenuous than petit-point. To date, the attempts to capture in literature the violence and passions of the actors in these frontier dramas have not quite fully succeeded. The mental weavings invariably wind up as mere cerebral embroidery, nothing more.

Over the long run, the most sustained range wars were fought between the cattle rustlers and the owners. Cattle stealing is at least as old as the time Jacob euchred his Uncle Laban out of his ring straked cattle, sheep, and goats. In many quarters in the West, and most especially in post-Civil War Texas, the concept of property rights in cattle was very vague, even after every steer had a potential home in Chicago via Kansas and was therefore worth gold. Any unbranded animal on the plains was fair game to whoever could get there first with an iron. These "mavericks," an accepted Anglo-American word straight out of Texas (Samuel Maverick had left four hundred head of cattle behind when he moved from Matagorda to San Antonio; the increase was not branded and roamed at will, and while other men kept up their cattle, here were Maverick's "mavericks" roaming all over the place, a beefy temptation to whoever wanted to cut out one or two for himself), presented an almost unparalleled opportunity to get into business without cash, capital, credit, or scruple.[1] Men availed themselves of that opportunity.

Cattle rustling had the dignity of history behind it. After all, Texans and Mexicans had raided each other's herds back and forth for a couple of decades before the Civil War. And then the big cattlemen—the cattle barons (a term they heartily disliked) of later years—didn't set an altogether good example for their employees, for in the days when the herds were being gathered after the Civil War, these men had a tendency to brand anything bovine they could get a rope on. The Texas system of placing a brand on every yearling found unbranded on the range quickly reached the northern plains. It was, of course, an axiom that an outfit never ate its own beef if a neighbor's was available.

The next step from "mavericking" was logical, just as there's a certain logic in the development of the bad actor who progresses from stealing from mother's purse to bootlegging to murder. After mavericking, it's not a far jump to branding any calf without a brand, even though it's obviously keeping company with a mother from another outfit, and, after that, to changing brands on cattle already claimed. Stories floated as far north as Montana of the far-

[1] Rena Maverick Green (ed.), *Samuel Maverick, Texan: 1803–1870*, 411–20. Dobie, *The Longhorns*, 43 ff.

stretching Texas spreads which began with no more invested capital than a running iron. In his Laramie *Boomerang*, in 1883, Bill Nye told how three years earlier a "guileless tenderfoot" had come to Wyoming "leading a single Texas steer and carrying a branding iron. Now he is the opulent possessor of six hundred head of fine cattle —the ostensible progeny of that one steer." [2] For that matter, the somewhat classic motion picture, *Red River*, otherwise a generally splendid representation, showed John Wayne coming into Texas' San Saba area with a small boy, a lone bull (a white-faced Hereford, but let that go), and a desire to be a cattleman; and then the movie jumps ten years ahead, and from that lone bull, in defiance of practically all we learned from biology, has emerged a herd of thousands. Whether the increase was due to hyperglandular activity on the part of the bull, or to fine-fingered, artful gulling on the part of *Señor* Wayne was not made clear. Quite seriously, it was no secret that many cowboys did a bit of cattle running of their own from strays flushed out of the brush.

Although, as has been seen, the frontier had its various criminal types ranging from the drifting ex-hide hunter to the Indian whiskey pedlar, the cattle thief was of necessity a cowboy, for he had to be an experienced cattle handler. Behind him might be a town brain, but the actual rustling was performed, as tobacco is selected in the cigarette advertisement, by men who knew their cattle best. To brand a calf overlooked in the spring roundup or to change the brand of your employer to your own was, if not easy, at least possible and profitable, though the path to riches might lead but to the grave, with time out en route to locate a live oak tree sufficiently sturdy and tall to hold a

[2] Gard, *Frontier Justice*, 123. Stuart, *Forty Years*, II, 167. Evan G. Barnard, *A Rider of the Cherokee Strip*, 92.

man's body a few inches off the ground. The country was measureless, with sufficient secluded spots to hide a small herd till you were ready to go to market with it. And the cowboy would never quite get used to the idea that any unbranded calf was not simply common property awaiting the brand of the first rider that came along.[3]

The larger ranch owners were as likely to be choused by their foremen as by some casual cowboy thief. Often the heads of the more extensive outfits lived in town during the winter and named foremen to look after their property. During the northern winters, about all a foreman would have to do would be to keep the ice broken on the watering holes, hold his men in line, and draw his salary. But under such isolated conditions, if he wanted to, the foreman could make some real inroads. Conditions could be made untenable for the dependable cowhands, who would then be replaced by cowboys of more criminal inclinations. The new staff would in turn ride the range— on the owner's horses and eating the chow the owner supplied—and wherever they found a calf following a cow that belonged to the man who was paying their wages, they could brand the calf and drive it away from its mother. Or, if the calf and mother stood steadfast, they could shoot the cow and leave it for the grey wolves and coyotes.[4]

Hiding the cattle presented no great problem. Every little swell in the land would be good for two or three head. Then there were creeks, canyons, arroyos, hills, and scrub timber. There are millions of cattle in the West, and yet so vast is its expanse that the eastern traveler driving, for instance, the two hundred miles from San Angelo to Alpine, Texas, in one of the hearts of the big ranch coun-

[3] Osgood, *The Day of the Cattleman*, 148–49, 33.
[4] Dale (ed.), *Frontier Trails: An Autobiography of Frank Canton*, 79–80.

try, can go the entire distance without seeing more than a handful of white-faced Herefords from his car window. He goes home disappointed, doubting that those millions of cattle really exist, believing that the country is over-rated cattlewise. There are millions of cattle, but what is difficult to comprehend from living in the more constricted sections is that there are even more millions of acres. But the cowboy realized this instinctively, and if he wanted to hide cattle that were branded illicitly, it was a problem that took a little thinking, but not so much that it was beyond his powers. Such rustling became so serious on some ranches—the XIT in Texas, for example—that any intruder found near the ranch line was shot first and questioned afterward, that is, if there were still any possibility of answers.[5]

Stealing unbranded cattle was much more popular and less dangerous than rebranding. Brand changing, in fact, has been considerably exaggerated in Western fiction, for it was a precarious procedure which, if botched, could shorten a man's life expectancy. The skill and ingenuity required to change a brand successfully was beyond the range of the average cowboy, and the rustlers who could change a brand so expertly that detection was nearly impossible were rather rare.

A brand on a young animal will generally hair over, but the hair will ruffle so as to show the brand. Should the rustler burn the old mark with a new brand, the new part of the brand would remain a clear scar. Or when the animal was skinned, the old brand on the flesh side of the hide would show more distinctly than the new brand.

[5] Haley, *The XIT Ranch of Texas*, 107. When in 1873 Rollie Burns accompanied a drive from Collin to Clay counties, Texas, his outfit had two men scouting either side of the trail for cattle from other spreads. Burns estimated that the four scouts drove between ten and fifty cattle a night into the herd he was trailing, taking care, however, to rustle no cattle from Jack or Palo Pinto county herds. Holden, *Rollie Burns*, 35–36.

Either way, you could denounce the owner as a rustler and expect your charge to stand up.

The average rustler carried only two tools, a piece of telegraph wire and a running iron. The easily concealed wire could be bent into any brand shape and be run into the old brand so perfectly that it was almost impossible to distinguish between a blend and an original. The running iron was a short iron rod with a handle at the grip end and the branding end so shaped that its tip could be turned to provide a tracing point which could be run over the old brand to alter it according to wish. The result was cruder than the telegraph-wire approach, so that on more difficult brands it left the rustler instead of the steer as the animal really branded. The regular branding iron was also used on occasion. It was applied to the hide through a scrap of saturated wool, burning through the material to obliterate the old brand and to reveal only a new brand. Placing a brand on a steer was akin to placing a wedding ring on a female's finger—you acknowledged to the world that you two somehow belonged together and that, further, you wanted no outside claimants. A branded steer, in other words, was figuratively under lock and key. A man who tampered with a brand could evoke the same sort of wrath as the man who violates a household, and a cattle owner who dealt summary justice to a rustler was no more liable for punishment than is the husband who kills the man caught bedding down with his once ever-loving wife.[6]

As the range cattle industry underwent its enormous expansion between 1879 and 1885, as the industry came to represent huge investments of capital, as the questions of water rights, grazing rights, and cattle ownership—questions which have troubled man throughout history—be-

[6] Haley, *The XIT Ranch of Texas*, 126. *Prose and Poetry*, 633. Velma Stevens Truett, *On the Hoof in Nevada*, 17–20.

came more intense, as it became evident that local, state, and federal governments—usually there was no local—could not assure each grazer his fair share of grass and water, and as it likewise became evident that the government could not furnish adequate law enforcement facilities, the cattleman abandoned that isolation which he had so treasured and which he had found so remunerative to turn to organization and co-operation. In came the cattlemen's associations—all-powerful combines often—to control grass and water rights, to organize roundups, to oversee branding, to check cattle diseases, to plan protection from Indians, thieves, and animals, and to return animals that had wandered off the home range. The associations employed brand inspectors who devoted full time to inspecting animals being driven from one region to another. And, finally, the associations exerted mounting pressure on the territorial and state legislatures to pass laws to the advantage of the cattleman.[7]

The best known organization in Texas was the Northwest Cattle Growers' Association, formed at Graham by a small group of ranchmen in 1877. By 1921, the association, which had meanwhile undergone two name changes and an enlarged membership, had recovered 110,000 animals or their value, exclusive of the incalculable amount saved through theft prevention.

Better known was the Wyoming Stock Growers' Association, organized under another name in late 1873. By 1883, there were 363 members owning two million head of stock. The work of the association was widespread, as was its influence, though we are here interested only in its relation to rustling. It was its war on thieves that provoked the notorious Johnson County War.

[7] Osgood, *The Day of the Cattleman*, 114–17. Dale, *The Range Cattle Industry*, 118.

The Association established protective devices to keep alert eyes on everybody in the cattle business. No one was above suspicion, least of all newcomers. Cowboys, like printers, are notorious job floaters, but the Association tried to keep track of each cowboy wherever he went. If a man picked up a record, he might as well leave Wyoming —there was small chance of escaping the blacklist. To control mavericking, the Association held one big roundup each season in which all members participated. Mavericks were driven in, offered for sale every ten days during the roundup, and sold to the highest bidder. Careful records were kept. The method left scant opportunity for the small independent to pick up a few strays from his neighbor's increase to aid him in getting established. Behind the Association soon stood the official sanction of the state of Wyoming, and this offered legal support that went unchallenged.

But eventually a challenge did arise, as the grangers— the northern equivalent of nesters—came in to homestead the land or to start small ranches. Here the cattle kings had competition, insignificant individually but an object of real concern in the aggregate. To meet it, the large rancher sought to exclude the farmer from the public lands, but the farmer–rancher fought back quite brazenly. Law enforcement soon broke down, for the farmers had the numbers, and no jury of farmers or—"Methodists, Grangers, and Anti-Stock," as one stockman put it—would convict a cattle thief, no matter how straightforward the evidence.[8]

[8] Osgood, *The Day of the Cattleman*, 119–21, 149–50, 154, 242–43. Quoting the federal census report of 1890, a contemporary points out that the Northeastern states, "which are supposed to be most civilized," have 1,600 criminals to the million people while Wyoming runs 25 per cent less, or 1,200 to the million. "As a matter of fact," he concludes, "there is less stealing and less lawlessness . . . on the plains of the West than in any other part of the world." A. S. Mercer, *The Banditti of the Plains*, 6–7.

With the grangers and small ranchers cutting up the range and with no longer any protection from the law, the ranchmen took matters into their own hands, precipitating the Wyoming Rustler's War of 1892, more commonly known as the Johnson County War. In the previous November, two suspected rustlers had been ambushed in Johnson County, with a federal deputy marshal being suspected. A large crowd had gathered at Buffalo, the county seat, to make threats against the marshal and the chief cattlemen of the region. Nothing had happened, except that tempers had waxed hotter as the spring of 1892 arrived.

Meanwhile, fifty armed men, rustlers perhaps, depending on the individual viewpoint, had taken over Buffalo with the complete sanction of county officials. They began to make demands, which the Association felt called upon to resist. Unfortunately, the resistance took the form of counteraction.

On April 4, 1892, the Association met in Cheyenne for a day. Whether what followed the next day was an official decision is unknown, but the tone of the meeting and the celerity with which things began to move were sufficient to convince the small farmer that the Association was responsible, an accusation to which the Association maintained silence.

During the afternoon of April 5, a special train arrived in Cheyenne from Denver, its equipment consisting of a chair car with tightly drawn curtains, a baggage car, three stock cars loaded with horses, a caboose, and a flat car with Studebaker wagons and camping supplies. No one was permitted near the train. In the night, it pulled out quietly for Casper, the nearest point to Johnson County. About the time of its arrival, the telegraph wires north of Casper were cut, leaving southern Wyoming to wonder what was going on in Johnson County.

At Casper, twenty-five Texas cowboys, recruited at so much a head from Denver, plus a number of leading members of the Association, as well as a "war" correspondent from the Chicago *Herald*, detrained from the curtained chair car, mounted the horses, and set off for Buffalo. Three days later, they besieged an isolated cabin containing two alleged rustlers, murdered them, and moved on toward Buffalo. Somehow the story of the killings had preceded them, so that on April 10 they were met by an irate citizenry a dozen miles outside Buffalo. Facing two hundred hostile anti-stockmen, including not a few hangers-on and "men about town," they retreated strategically to a deserted ranch.

Word got back to Cheyenne that a number of Wyoming's leading citizens were endangered by an angry mob, whereupon the acting Governor wired President Benjamin Harrison to order out federal troops from Fort McKinney, twenty-five miles from Buffalo. The troops arrived on April 13, in time to put down the "war" and, most important, to stop a movable platform, loaded with dynamite, from being pushed against the cabin containing the besieged cattlemen. The cattlemen were then taken under troop escort back to Cheyenne to avoid vigilante action.

What would have happened to the cattlemen if they had been taken to Johnson County for trial is rather clear, but that never came about, as Johnson County was too poor to stand the cost of a trial. The two material witnesses to the murder were arrested by a federal marshal for selling whiskey to Indians and shipped—or exiled—to Omaha, and the district court at Cheyenne decided that, since Johnson County could not pay for a trial, the only thing left to do was to turn the men loose on their own recognizance. The Texas cowboys were mailed back to Fort Worth.[9]

The outcome did nothing to stop rustling in Wyoming. And Wyoming was just one of the areas affected. Granville Stuart emphasized the plight when he pointed out that Montana stockmen had 35 million dollars worth of property scattered over 75,000 square miles of practically uninhabited country. How could you protect your property under such conditions? The only way, it seemed, was to make the penalty so severe that only the most madcap would dare the risk. Stuart estimated in 1893 that Montana cattlemen suffered a 3 per cent loss from rustlers.[10]

The animosity between the homesteader and the cattleman is understandable. The cattleman had come into Indian-infested territory and had risked his life to build up an area. To his mind, as one stockman pointed out, he had overcome obstacles "far greater than those of the Pilgrim Fathers, for the Indians of Massachusetts had no kindly disposed Indian Bureau to supply them with the most up-to-date firearms." [11] And now, having won over the land, he was being defeated by men who were either outright thieves or who cut up the public domain with legal sanction, which to the range cattleman was just another form of robbery. The Indian had made a better opponent: you could shoot him. But the nester was a varmint supported by federal law, and he swarmed in like a plague of red ants.

[9] Osgood, *The Day of the Cattleman*, 247–53. Gard, *Frontier Justice*, 121–45. Mercer's *The Banditti of the Plains*, originally written in 1894 by a prominent Western educator, places all of the blame on the cattlemen for trying to treat the grangers and small cattlemen like so many uncollectivized *muzhiks* and for invading their personal property rights.

[10] *Forty Years*, II, 195.

[11] Osgood, *The Day of the Cattleman*, 249.

You had, too, a clash of types. The ranch society had been a purely masculine society of longhorn steers, hard riding cowboys, boots, spurs, big hats, six-guns, branding irons, and other paraphernalia as exciting as that carried by any Prussian soldier. The farmer brought his wife and children to clutter the scene, along with such despicable "squaw tools" as hoes and plows. He also brought schools, churches, and Sunday schools to compete with saloons, dance halls, and gaming tables. The cowboy was plainly contemptuous of most of this. He did not fear the nester, a lack of feeling which was not exactly mutual, for the nester saw the cowboy as a member of a wild and reckless breed of men who feared neither God nor man, carried guns, fought regularly, never attended church, and probably did other things too evil to mention though not to contemplate.

Inevitably, contact between the two groups grew, and as it grew suspicion lessened. The cowboy fell in love with the nester's daughter and found her people to be good after all. The children of the newcomers, awed by the swashbuckling cowboy, immediately made him their hero. Likewise, the granger learned that the range rider could mend a fence and in other ways not be thoroughly depraved. And so it was that the longhorn frontier which the cowboy had called his own made way for a new factor, the small farmer and the fenced-in range.[12]

A darker picture in the gallery of range wars is that depicting the conflict between the sheepman and the cattleman. The frontier cattleman had feared and hated the rustler and had disliked the nester, but for the *pastores* he had only condemnation and an almost unholy contumely. One old herder, who had kept sheep in Scotland, com-

[12] Dale, "The Cow Country in Transition," *Mississippi Valley Historical Review*, Vol. XXIV, No. 1 (June, 1937), 3–20.

plained that back home when he brought down his flock, the people would exclaim, "Here comes the noble shepherd and his flock." Out West, he continued, they said, "Here comes that d—d sheepherder and his bunch of woolies!" [13] A cowboy might marry a squaw, but associate with a shepherd—never! If you wanted to provoke a fight, call him a sheepherder—not a shepherd, for that was a term he didn't use. The only pleasant thing you can say about the sheep–cattle feud is that it was simple and straightforward. The two groups just plain did not like each other and had no intention of changing. The cowboy would even quote a bit of *Ezekiel* to back him up:

Woe be to shepherds of Israel! . . . Seemeth it a small thing unto you to have eaten up the good pasture, but ye must tread down with your feet the residue of your pastures? And to have drunk of the deep waters, but ye must foul the residue with your feet?

But cattlemen, who fought with weapons other than scriptural, felt they had all the rights of priority. They had arrived behind the buffalo and ahead of the sheep, and anything that came after the cattlemen was an interloper. And sheep most of all, for "everything is front of sheep is eaten, and everything behind is killed." [14] Such a contention, though prejudiced, is indisputable to a cattleman. When sheep enter into a pasture, they graze grass closely to the earth, even to the roots. Cattle, the cowman claims, cannot live where sheep have grazed. The sheepmen could argue that government land belonged as much to sheep as to cattle, that a range can serve both sheep and cattle to the mutual advantage of both, that

[13] Quoted in Charles Wayland Towne and Edward Norris Wentworth, *Shepherds Empire*, 256.

[14] Towne and Wentworth, *Shepherds Empire*, 186. Clara M. Love, "History of the Cattle Industry in the Southwest," *Southwestern Historical Quarterly*, Vol. XX, No. 1 (July, 1916), 13.

sheep won't eat the same long, rank grass that cattle will but will eat other, shorter grass that cattle cannot reach, and that sheep will eat away weeds, giving grass an opportunity to grow for the cattle that can follow. But such arguments require a logical approach for acceptance, and the cattleman just flat didn't think the Lord had intended the West for sheep.[15]

Furthermore, the longhorn was a wild creature needing long grass and plenty of water. He had to be tended by a man on horseback who understood his nature and could bring his moods and habits under subjection. But what was the sheep?—a domesticated animal subsisting on short grass and weeds and, except in the hottest weather, requiring little water. And the sheepherders, who were worse than sheep—little better than a "pelon" dog, according to one observer, rode no horse, but either walked or rode a donkey. For helpers, they used a dog. Were such creatures men!

Certainly the cattlemen didn't treat the sheepmen with the dignity due fellow men. They tried intimidation, and if that failed, they tried violence. Next came murder, either for the sheepmen or their flocks. As public sympathy was generally with the cattlemen, a sheepman had no recourse at law if his herder were killed or his sheep driven off the range. Although fiction tells a different story, the cowboy showed no inherent sportsmanship in dealing with his enemy, being careful usually to outnumber the one herder on foot with five to ten cowboys on horseback. Numerous narratives could be told of individual attacks on herders, but the Graham-Tewksbury quarrel will suffice as an example.

The Grahams and Tewksburys had hated each other

[15] T. F. Havins, "Sheepmen–Cattlemen Antagonisms on the Texas Frontier," *West Texas Historical Association Year Book*, Vol. XXVIII (October, 1942), 11–12. Winifred Kupper (ed.), *Texas Sheepman; The Reminiscences of Robert Maudslay*, 39–40.

back in Texas, and a move to Arizona for both families did nothing to diminish this hatred. Although both groups were primarily cattlemen, the Tewksbury family began to run sheep on the range claimed by the Grahams. From then on, it was a case of the Hatfields and McCoys, with both sides heavily armed and prepared to shoot first.

Open conflict erupted when eight cowboys rode toward the isolated Newton ranch in the Tonto Basin of central Arizona, where they expected to be welcomed. But the Tewksbury brothers with five cronies were holed up inside, and in ten seconds three cowboys were dead and two others wounded. Within a month, the cowboys had laid siege to the Tewksbury ranch house, killing John Tewksbury. After that, retaliation followed retaliation. Within five years, all peaceable ranchers had been driven from the country, and twenty-six cattlemen and six sheepmen had been killed. This episode, incidentally, was the basis for Zane Grey's *To the Last Man* and Dane Coolidge's *The Men Killers*.

Five years didn't see the end of the bitterness, for it spread northward and merged with the general fight between sheepmen and cattlemen that continued into the twentieth century. Along the upper reaches of Wyoming's Green River, it took the form of a masked group, organized by the cattlemen, who attacked four sheep camps simultaneously. The group blindfolded the herders, tied them to trees, and spent the remainder of the night clubbing to death eight thousand head of sheep.[16] Nowhere was the violence of the Great Plains more vicious than in the sheep–cattle feuds. And oddly, it is a phase which

[16] Havins, "Sheepmen–Cattlemen Antagonisms on the Texas Frontier," *West Texas Historical Association Year Book*, Vol. XXVIII (October, 1942), 11–12. Towne and Wentworth, *Shepherds Empire*, 182–91. Gard, *Frontier Justice*, 62–77.

Erwin E. Smith: Library of Congress

CHUCK WAGON UP FROM RED RIVER. This typical outfit
carried bedding, grub, cooking gear for all hands.

Erwin E. Smith: Library of Congress

TAKE YOUR PICK. The cowboy is looking at the calf on the left, but the horse is eyeing the one on the right.

historians have been content to mention in passing, while fiction writers have gone little deeper.

A greater menace than sheep was the introduction of barbed wire. Here, where violence was insufficient, the cattleman ran into a problem which did more than pit man against man; here the open range closed down permanently. More than anything else, the range cattleman wanted room, but the barbed wire came to enclose range, waterhole, and trail. In a way, it was a fitting product to terminate the range cattle days, for like the frontier and its cowboy inhabitants, barbed wire was savage, unrefined, and hard—and it made the Great Plains finally fit for settlement.

Barbed wire had its own chapter in the range wars, and before the barbed wire advocates won, fence cutting skirmishes starting in Texas reached all the way north to Montana. As in the other range wars, people were killed, property destroyed, business crippled, and peaceful citizens alienated from one another. Men cut fences because their cattle were thirsty and the tanks were enclosed, or because they desired the good grass now out of bounds, or because the large ranching syndicates had fenced in whole counties, thus pitting the little man in the age-old battle against the gigantic, hated corporation—the Spur Ranch, for instance, erected a drift fence in 1884–1885 that strung out for fifty-seven miles, while an old Two Circle Bar cowboy told of seeing ten wagonloads of barbed wire in the middle 1880's in transit from Colorado City, Texas to the Matador ranch—or because the fence had thrown a cowboy out of work, or because as a rustler, fence cutting was necessary for the safe conduct of his stolen cattle, or because some men fenced land to which they had no right, or, finally, because barbed wire cut animals and exposed them to infection.

But barbed wire had come to stay, to turn the range cattle industry into stock farming and to improve herds by making selective breeding possible. Quickly, the men who initially opposed barbed wire became its ardent supporters as they obtained legal rights to the land over which they had been operating and as they observed their herds' improvement.[17] Today the hatred and bloodshed are forgotten, and fine ranches and farms and cattle all over the West stand as testimony to the use of barbed wire and the legal right to call the land property.

Finally, the story of the range wars and of the lawless is told in the vigilante committee. The cowboy had fought the rustler and had been a rustler, had assaulted the sheepman and had been one, had resisted the nester and had married his daughter, had built wire fences and had cut them, and had victimized Kansas cowtowns and had been victimized by them. Here, in vigilante lore, the cowboy continued his dual role of being all things to the American folk—here the cowboy was both executioner as well as the executed.

Lynching, as is well known, is an extralegal action taken because the law is inadequate, because the legal machinery refuses to operate, or because men's passions run high. Aside from the South, where the approach was primarily racial, nowhere was lynch justice more swift, certain, or flourishing than on the cattleman's frontier. Owen Wister recognized this fact when he made the climax of *The Virginian* a sundown gun battle between the

---

[17] Cox, *Historical and Biographical Record*, 45. Webb, *The Great Plains*, 280–313. Earl E. Hayter, "Barbed Wire Fencing—A Prairie Invention," *Agricultural History*, Vol. XIII, No. 4 (October, 1939), 202–203. R. D. Holt, "The Introduction of Barbed Wire Into Texas and the Fence Cutting War," *West Texas Historical Association Year Book*, Vol. VI (June, 1930), 70–74. Holden, *The Spur Ranch*, 64–65. Williams, *The Big Ranch Country*, 55.

Virginian and a horse thief arising from the actions of a vigilante committee.

Perhaps the fact that human life was not considered very valuable on the frontier made it difficult to convict a man for murder. Taking a human life was accepted almost casually, like a routine automobile accident today. The ubiquitous six-shooter and the absent courtroom undoubtedly aided such an attitude. Lynch law was directed more against social crimes than against crimes against the person. The most serious transgression was the theft of a horse, and was usually punishable by hanging. There was hardly such a thing as an extenuating circumstance for a horse thief. On the other hand, a cattle thief could get off fairly lightly at times, for after all, cattle were merely property, while a man's life could depend on his horse.

Granville Stuart, a leading spirit in the Montana vigilante work, tells the story of a Billy Downs who was suspected of selling whiskey to Indians, stealing horses, and killing cattle. Because he was married and had his wife with him, he was let off with a stern warning, which, however, made no difference in his behavior. One July 4, the vigilantes called on Downs and ordered him from his house. After first refusing, he emerged in company with an unsavory character known as California Ed. Both men pleaded guilty to stealing horses from the Indians, but denied ever stealing from white men. On the other hand, their pen contained twenty-six horses with white men's brands—not their own—on them. They further claimed that the quantity of dried meat on the premises was buffalo, despite the fact that the last buffalo in the area had disappeared two years previously. A freshly salted bale of hides bore the brand of the Fergus Stock Company. The two men were carried out to a near-by grove and hanged.

In another instance, this one involving a woman, the

vigilantes suspected the woman, Ella Watson, or "Cattle Kate," and her cohort, a saloonkeeper named Jim Averill, of putting their brand on every maverick they could locate. In the summer of 1889, they swung from a pine.[18] Owen Wister, incidentally, mentioned Cattle Kate in *The Virginian.*

Typical of vigilante activity was the following warning posted in Las Vegas, New Mexico, in 1880:

To MURDERERS, CONFIDENCE MEN, THIEVES:

The citizens of Las Vegas have tired of robbery, murder, and other crimes that have made this town a byword in every civilized community. They have resolved to put a stop to crime even if in attaining that end they have to forget the law, and resort to a speedier justice than it will afford. All such characters are, therefore, notified that they must either leave this town or conform themselves to the requirement of law, or they will be summarily dealt with. The flow of blood MUST and SHALL be stopped in this community, and the good citizens of both the old and new towns have determined to stop it, if they have to HANG by the strong arm of FORCE every violator of the law in this country.

VIGILANTES [19]

In American frontier history, new regions in the process of development have generally been theaters of lawlessness and conflict before their populations have had time to become assimilated and reasonably homogeneous.

[18] Genevieve Yost, "History of Lynchings in Kansas," *Kansas Historical Quarterly,* Vol. II, No. 2 (May, 1933), 182–97. Stuart, *Forty Years,* II, 206. John Clay, *My Life on the Range,* 272–73. Charles A. Guernsey, *Wyoming Cowboy Days,* 91.

[19] Otero, *My Life on the Frontier, 1864–1882,* 205–206. Vigilance groups did not always enjoy a reputation for justice. In Socorro, New Mexico, for instance, the vigilantes hanged a Mexican monte dealer because they were incensed at his two employers, even though those employers were paying the vigilantes 12 dollars a day to keep their monte tables open. Jim McIntire, *Early Days in Texas,* 142–43.

At the close of the Civil War, one of the graver problems facing the undeveloped West was that of controlling its population. In rough areas accessible to border settlements, the Western desperado would establish his base of operations against the more law-abiding citizenry. Against such, a court of justice had little power, so that the six-gun or rope came to be considered superior to judicial procedure. It was certainly more expeditious. The amazing development of the West following Appomattox was so swift that courts of justice simply were unable to keep up with frontier progress. In 1877, Texas alone had five thousand men on its wanted list.[20] As Theodore Roosevelt pointed out, "the fact of such scoundrels being able to ply their trade with impunity for any length of time can only be understood if the absolute wildness of our land is taken into account."[21]

By 1885, most of the frontier areas of the Great Plains had passed the worst stages of outlawry, but committees were still operating on the northern plains at a later date. In 1888, Roosevelt told how "notorious bullies and murderers have been taken out and hung, while the bands of horse thieves have been regularly hunted down and destroyed in pitched fights by parties of armed cowboys."[22]

The story of the cowboy and his relationship to the vigilante committee is simple enough. If he turned rustler, he could expect lynch law, with his former range riding colleagues as his executioners. If he turned desperado, he could expect the same fate, or be short-circuited, as was Billy the Kid, by a bullet from ambush. Western fiction

[20] Rister, "Outlaws and Vigilantes of the Southern Plains, 1865–1885," *Mississippi Valley Historical Review*, Vol. XIX (1932–1933), 537, 544–45.
[21] "Sheriff's Work on a Ranch," *Century Magazine*, Vol. XXXVI, No. 1 (May–October, 1888), 40.
[22] "Ranch Life in the Far West," *Century Magazine*, Vol. XXXV, No. 4 (February, 1888), 505.

may have overstressed the themes of the lawless West and the bloody range wars, but there is no arguing but that prevailing conditions were bad enough. The best statement that can be made about the cowboy in all of this, a statement that will withstand historical investigation, is that he was not the worst offender and that he was more often on the side of the law than at odds with it.

8. The Other Frontiers

WILLIAM F. CODY was as vain as a woman at Easter, as unprincipled as a race track tout, and as congenital a liar as the man who wrote those all-inclusive patent medicine ads of the nineteenth century. Cody—or Buffalo Bill—has also come to be a symbol for the Wild West, proving again that there is considerable value and significance to any liar–promoter provided he can perform his dubious services in a grandiloquent manner. Buffalo Bill could do just that.

Born in Iowa in 1846, he grew up at his father's frontier trading post in Kansas, where he played with Indian children and talked with soldiers and bullwhackers. He met William H. Russell, the freighter, who let the boy accompany him while he assembled and dispatched his pic-

121

turesque freighting trains. By the time he was eleven years old, he was acting as messenger for Alexander Majors. As a boy of fourteen, he carried mail from Leavenworth to St. Joseph to be put aboard the pony express.

Cody won his Buffalo Bill sobriquet while killing buffaloes for the Union Pacific building crew in Kansas. Within seventeen months—by his count—he killed 4,280 of them. Like ol' Pharaoh's daughter's account of the bullrush adoption, that statement has to be taken on faith, as no auditor certified the books on Cody. For a time, he served as an army scout for Generals Sheridan and Carr. In 1877, he and his partner, Major Frank M. North, bought a range and ranch at the head of the South Dismal River in Nebraska, and established the CN brand. After six weeks in the saddle during a roundup, Cody decided that cowboy life as such was not for him, and thereafter he left his ranching business to his partner. Best known was his long run with his Wild West Show,[1] which took a sampling of a reasonably authentic West to the tamer world under the magnetic leadership of a reasonably authentic and certainly many-faceted Western type. Buffalo Bill became the symbol of the West, and with good reason, for he had touched nearly every frontier of the Great Plains during his career, being a freighter, Indian scout, Indian fighter, soldier, buffalo hunter, and cowboy. About the only things he missed out on were Western railroad construction, which he fringed, and the mining frontier. In a world that hadn't yet learned to adulate and idolize spoiled sports stars, clinging crooners, candlelight

[1] Richard J. Walsh, *The Making of Buffalo Bill*, 27, 42, 67, 120 ff., 206. William F. Cody, *An Autobiography of Buffalo Bill*, 118. Frank S. Hastings, the long-time manager of the S.M.S. ranch, said that romance had made of Cody "almost everything that the West, in its wildest woolliness, is capable of," but added that he was one of the world's few notables he would trouble to "look up" whenever they came to town. Hastings, *A Ranchman's Recollections*, 106–109.

piano players, and shirtless cinema stars, he was a man for the mob, male and female alike.

The point in giving this much space to such an exaggerated character is that Buffalo Bill personifies in a sense the West of the period of the cowboy. There was the range cattle frontier, which we have been at a little pains to delineate. But in addition, there were other contemporary frontiers which conditioned the cowboy's activities and outlooks. Although a case could be made demonstrating that each of the frontiers had little or no relation to the Texas longhorn—that the cowboy had nothing to do with the Western stagecoach except to ride in one occasionally, that his only connection with a freighting train was to pass one as he trailed his herd across the plains, that he trespassed on the mining frontier, or vice versa, only when he trailed his cattle into Deadwood or some other mining camp looking for a buyer, that he rode the range with a frontier army between him and the Indian reservations, and so on—actually what the other frontiers experienced and achieved became of vital importance in extending the cattleman's frontier across the open pasture lands of the West.

As a matter of historical record, the conquering of the High Plains began in the first years of the nineteenth century with such exploration expeditions as those of Lewis and Clark, Zebulon M. Pike, and Stephen H. Long. Tales of beaver in quantity brought on a migration of trappers who became known as the "mountain men." In the Southwest, meanwhile, traders had begun to push out over what became the Santa Fe Trail to develop commerce with first the Spaniards and then their successors, the Mexicans. The area soon became crisscrossed with not very well defined trails, as men went wherever there was profit.

Farmers and homemakers came, pushing toward the Pacific Coast and the Oregon country—the trail of the prairie schooners, the Oregon Trail. But the group which really shattered the quiet of the Plains was the miners, who sought precious metals and who found them in quantity in such later states as California, Colorado, Nevada, Montana, Wyoming, Arizona, and the Dakotas.

The result of all this was that the typical Westerner was, like the typical American, actually nonexistent, and the typical Western town, though decidedly different from its Eastern counterpart, was most likely composed of a conglomeration of frontier types who had come west for any one of a half-dozen reasons. Theodore Roosevelt described such a town in the 1880's:

A town in the cattle country, when for some cause is thronged with men from the neighborhood around, always presents a picturesque sight on the wooden sidewalks of the broad, dusty streets . . . hunters in their buckskin shirts and fur caps, greasy and unkept, but with resolute faces and sullen, watchful eyes, that are ever on the alert; teamsters, surly and self-contained, with slouch hats and great cowhide boots; stage-drivers, their faces seamed by hardship and exposure during their long drives with every kind of team, through every kind of country, and in every kind of weather . . . trappers and wolfers, whose business is to poison wolves . . . silent sheep-herders, with cast-down faces. . . .[2]

No other factor contributed as compellingly to the settlement of the West as the discovery of precious metals and the boom conditions which invariably ensued. Under the spell of possible fabulous strikes, men dared, and in daring pushed back and subdued the Indian, founded towns and cities, established markets for produce, thereby

[2] "Ranch Life in the Far West," *Century Magazine,* Vol. XXXV, No. 4 (February, 1888), 501.

encouraging ranching and farming, and created a demand for transportation and communications facilities that couldn't go unheeded.

Outside of California, the first gold boom in the West hit in Colorado in 1859, just on the eve of the Civil War, bringing an estimated 100,000 people across the plains, most of whom went home disappointed. But not all went, and still others arrived as later news told of an incredibly rich silver strike—the Comstock Lode—in Nevada. About the same time, James and Granville Stuart discovered paying gold in Montana, and other gold deposits were found there through 1864. Granville Stuart, of course, is one of the more revered cattlemen frequently cited in this book. His story furnishes but one illustration, one statistic, of the importance of gold to the cattle industry, because gold in Montana brought in Anglo-Americans to settle to the rear of the Indian barrier and thereby hasten the occupation of the more northerly plains by Texas cattle.

In Montana, gold played out rather quickly, as it did also in Wyoming. But the importance of gold in these territories lies not in its richness nor in its permanence, but in the fact that the presence of gold advertised the area and attracted men like a magnet. And whenever men came, some always remained, leaving a nucleus for permanent settlement. And for men restless enough to have come in the first place, was there a more suitable manner of living than vagabond trafficking in transient cattle?

The most fabulous mining town would have to be either Deadwood in the Dakotas or Tombstone, Arizona. Deadwood is perhaps best known for the characters who infested (a precise word in this instance) it. Calamity Jane was one, Wild Bill Hickok was another, and Richard Clark was a third, and if his name as such is unfamiliar, you may know him as "Deadwood Dick," about whom

Beadle and Adams published 130 novels in twenty years, none of which, incidentally, let facts stand in the way of a good story.[3]

Named by a waggish prospector who was told by the army that the only stone he'd ever find in those parts would be his tombstone, Tombstone was a converging point for at least three "last" frontiers—mining, cattle, and Indian. This was Geronimo's Apache country, and the Apaches were the last of their race to be subdued. This was the country of the unforgettable Wyatt Earp, fresh from carving a gun-fighting reputation as a marshal in Ellsworth, Wichita, and Dodge City; of Curly Bill Brocius, a rustler thus far beyond the descriptive powers of the better Western novelists; Doc Holliday, "lean, consumptive, sardonic and deadly"; and foppish Bat Masterson, former Dodge City sheriff once fined 8 dollars for shooting a citizen through the lung. Tombstone was a town loaded with luxuries, with jammed stores, with the inevitable honky-tonks and saloons, and with all the violence for which the West is notorious. It was close by the Mexican border, which facilitated rustling in both directions. At no place were the mining and cattle frontiers more closely associated, nor more closely attuned to the "badman" theme, than in Tombstone.[4]

Arizona with its painted deserts, bare mountains, organ cactus, cerulean skies, and vast vistas has long been a particularly favorite setting for fiction writers and movie producers. The tales emanating from historic Tombstone haven't discouraged that tendency in the least.

[3] Albert Johannsen, The House of Beadle and Adams and Its Dime and Nickel Novels, II, 358–59.

[4] Rufus Kay Wyllys, Arizona: The History of a Frontier State, 220, 176. J. J. Wagoner, History of the Cattle Industry in Southern Arizona, 1540–1940, 104 ff. Otero, My Life on the Frontier, 1864–1882, 217. Stuart N. Lake, Wyatt Earp: Frontier Marshal, 242. Wellman, Glory, God and Gold, 376. Gard, The Chisholm Trail, 237, 254.

Sharing almost equal importance with mining in the development of the West was the transportation frontier, both before the railroad and after. The railroad, of course, was vital to the development of the range cattle industry, as has been reiterated incidentally along this way. It and its later handmaiden, the refrigerator car, were the two products of the Industrial Revolution that made the trail drives financially feasible, that brought Texas beef to metropolitan markets, and that switched American meat-eating habits from a pork to a beef standard. Actually, other than economic, the chief contribution of the railroad to the making of the individual cowboy came through providing the Kansas cowtown terminals for him to relax in after the long drive. Oddly, the railroad story, for all its epic qualities, has been barely noticed in fiction, except to introduce an unfeeling railroad director from the East as a villain or an occasional railroad detective as a hero. Zane Grey tried to depict the Union Pacific saga in his *The U. P. Trail* with the usual commercial success and the just-as-usual lack of artistry.

From a strictly frontier standpoint, the pre-railroad story of Western transportation serves better to focus the time picture as it relates to other processes contemporary with the era of the range-and-trail cowboy. The crest of the freighting era may have preceded the rise of the range cattle industry, but in the West of the cowboy the now powerful railroad, despite its reticulation of routes, still missed many a Western community, leaving wagon freighting as the cattleman's contact with civilization. In our period, the freighting industry more nearly conditioned the cowman's material outlook than did the Iron Horse.

After California was settled, stagecoach service between the East and California became a necessity, so

Congress provided for an overland mail service to California four years before Fort Sumter was fired on. John Butterfield and associates received a contract to carry mail twice weekly in a southerly semicircle from St. Louis to San Francisco, looping down through the Ozarks across Texas and into southern California before turning back northward to San Francisco. The contract called for 600,000 dollars a year, and it was worth all of that. Twenty-five days were scheduled for the trip each way. By the middle 1860's, stagecoaching was at its apex, after which the railroad began to make its extending presence felt.

It wasn't an easy trip. The white-oak Concord coach, which was used almost exclusively, provided for nine passengers—three with their back to the driver, three in a center seat, and three others facing forward. Upholstery was usually a russet leather. Heavy, canvas-duck side curtains decorated the top of each window. In the absence of steel springs, the body rode suspended on two leather thoroughbraces extending lengthwise of the coach and attached at each end to a standard protruding up from the axle.[5] The effect, as Mark Twain commented, was to make of the coach "a great swinging and swaying" thing.[6]

Staging companies realized the picturesqueness of their operation, and did their best to live up to it. Besides the semi-sumptuousness of the coach's body, both inside and out, care was taken to employ drivers who were every bit as skilled with their span of four or six horses as a cowboy with his mustang. Whenever possible, all horses were of the same shade and tapered in size from the wheelers to the leaders. Spirited horses were selected, horses that would respond to the lordly driver's call for a dash into

[5] LeRoy R. Hafen, *The Overland Mail, 1849–1869*, 87–96, 295–96, 306. William Swilling Wallace, "Short–Line Staging in New Mexico," *New Mexico Historical Review*, Vol. XXVI, No. 2 (April, 1951), 94.
[6] *Roughing It*, 5.

and out of the stations as the local populace cheered lustily.[7]

Along the Western stage routes, the companies erected (which is almost too dignified a word for what was actually assembled) crude stations of wood or adobe at ten- to fifteen-mile intervals. Here were food and shelter for people and animals. Likely as not, the agent in charge of the station was wanted by a half-dozen vigilante committees. A "district agent" supervised each two hundred miles of the route. He differed from his subordinates only in being quicker with his pistols, for he was the man who enforced discipline in an undisciplined area.

The motion picture screen and Western fiction abound with scenes involving the frontier stagecoach. Two themes are played almost to the exclusion of all others. The more frequent is the stagecoach robbery; the other is the Indian attack. Neither theme is particularly overdrawn. Though the regularity of such attacks may be exaggerated and though invariably the robbers are high-heeled cowboy types with their Stetson brims rolled high, moving in to intercept a payroll or a valuable gold shipment from a nearby mine, the stagecoaches feared the holdup men and the Indians more than other hazards of the road or of economics. At one period, the Deadwood stage—only recently celebrated in gay popular song, and by a feminine woman at that—was held up so regularly that it became almost impossible to transport gold out of the Black Hills. Most highwaymen did their job with an organization and efficiency that almost invites respect. One man would hold the reins, a second would cover the passengers with his gun, and a third would rob each victim. Finally, the express companies resorted to building special treasure coaches lined with bulletproof steel and

[7] Hafen, *The Overland Mail*, 306, 309–310. Twain, *Roughing It*, 15.

with guards inside, their guns pointed toward possible harassing "road agents." But even then, as late as 1877, a Deadwood newspaper opined ruefully that "We have again to repeat the now hackneyed phrase 'the stage coach has been robbed' three miles below Battle Creek." [8]

Indian attacks were about as bad. For a four-months' period ending August 15, 1867, the Post Office admitted that the Overland stage had been robbed by the Indians of 350 head of stage stock. In addition, the Indians had burned twelve stations, along with large amounts of hay and grain, destroyed three coaches, wounded several passengers, and killed thirteen employees. [9]

The passing of the stagecoach in general was a story of sudden death. The railroad built into an area, and the "magnificent Concord Coach" became the "terrible rattling stage." [10] Thus Denver lost its need for stage routes when the Union Pacific came chugging through in the latter 1860's. The same story can be told all over the West— in Hays City, when the Kansas Pacific moved in; in Sacramento, when the Central Pacific reached such former stage depots as Cisco; and in northern Utah, when the Union Pacific and the Central Pacific held their not-too-tender Wedding of the Rails. And yet the West was spacious, and the population in spots remained sparse, so that in some areas, even as far east as Texas, there were still some stage routes operating as late as the twentieth century. But by and large, the day of the stagecoach ended a full decade before the cowboy quit trailing his herd to Kansas, and the name of Wells Fargo was on its way to becoming legendary, while the more important contemporary names of Butterfield and of Ben Holladay, the first

[8] Dick, *Vanguards of the Frontier*, 335-37.
[9] Hafen, *The Overland Mail*, 320.
[10] *Ibid.*, 321-27.

Erwin E. Smith: Library of Congress

SLAUGHTERING MEAT FOR CAMP. Five hands of half
a century ago get ready for a steak dinner.

Erwin E. Smith: Library of Congress

TONSORIAL SERVICE. As it was done at
a line camp, "one hundred miles from nowhere."

real stagecoach king of the West, were on their way to being forgotten by all except specialists in things Western.

Although not as colorful as stagecoaching, freighting, an old story to eastern frontiersmen, was even more important to the development of the West. Freighting had been carried on since the first days when the Yankees had exchanged goods with the Spanish by way of the Santa Fe Trail. There had been some freighting after gold was discovered in California, though most supplies were still brought in by boat. The Mormons had their freighting organization. But the great upsurge of western freighting came as a result of the Mormon War in 1857, when Russell, Majors, and Waddell, with Alexander Majors, a Methodist minister of sorts, as the driving spirit, were employed to haul supplies to the 2,500 soldiers sent in to quell the disturbances. The freighting firm used 6,000 mules, 47,000 oxen, 5,000 wagons, and a large number of men in fulfilling its contract; and freighting had come to the West as a real industry.[11]

Organizing a full-fledged train for crossing the plains represented careful planning and gathering. A train consisted of about twenty-five wagons, each carrying about seven thousand pounds, pulled by six yoke of oxen, which had the advantage of being able to subsist off the grass along the way, thereby eliminating the necessity for carrying grain and dry fodder. Included in the score or more of wagons were a mess wagon and sometimes an office wagon. At one end of the train rode the wagon master, or boss, while his assistant watched the train from the opposite end. Third in command was the commissary, who acted as business manager and issued provisions. A fourth person, usually a boy, such as the young Buffalo Bill, car-

[11] Louis Pelzer, *The Cattleman's Frontier*, 26–27. Walker D. Wyman, "Bull-Whacking: A Prosaic Profession Peculiar to the Great Plains," *New Mexico Historical Review*, Vol. VII, No. 2 (October, 1932), 307.

ried messages from one official to another, or from one train to another.

The bullwhackers drove the teams. Usually between twenty-five and forty-five years old, they wore the Western broad-brimmed hat, the red or blue flannel shirt, and trousers tucked into boot tops. At hand were the inevitable Bowie knife, pistol, and shotgun. Bullwhackers were proud of their vocabularies, having a range of profanity that was well-nigh intolerable.[12] They were proud, too, of their abilities with the bull whip—a five-pound or better lash fifteen to twenty feet long, tipped with a buckskin popper, and attached to eighteen or twenty inches of polished hickory handle. To wield such a whip took enormous strength, and to crack it like a gunshot meant that in the democratic prairie country the wielder belonged to the aristocracy.[13]

And so, amid the cracking of a score of whips, sounding for all the world like a picket line performing night harassing fire, the wagons would begin to roll out about dawn on their daily fifteen-mile or more journey. The train stretched across the prairie all the way to the horizon, the glaring white of their canvas against their brightly painted hulls giving the appearance of a fleet of caravels under full sail, the wheels rending the air with their high-frequency screeching, despite generous appli-

[12] LeRoy R. Hafen and Carl Coke Rister, *Western America*, 494. Dick, *Vanguards of the Frontier*, 349–50. Wyman, "Bull-Whacking: A Prosaic Profession Peculiar to the Great Plains," *New Mexico Historical Review*, Vol. VII, No. 2 (October, 1932), 306. Any profanity or other vulgarity would exist in spite of owner Majors, who extracted from each new employee a pledge "not to use profane language, not to get drunk, not to gamble, not to treat animals cruelly, and not to do anything else that is incompatible with the conduct of a gentleman."

[13] Wyman, "Bull-Whacking: A Prosaic Profession Peculiar to the Great Plains," *New Mexico Historical Review*, Vol. VII, No. 2 (October, 1932), 299–301. Harold E. Briggs, "Early Freight and Stage Lines in Dakota," *North Dakota Historical Quarterly*, Vol. III (1928–1929), 258–60.

cation of resin, tallow, and pitch, whips cracking, team-sters' coarse voices demanding "gee-ho" and "ho-haw," and horses snorting and oxen grunting. A picturesque sight indeed, but also an important commercial sight, each two-ton wagon with its long tongue of a dozen feet or more carrying the necessities of life to the men who needed them and, almost as important, to the men who would pay for them, supplying every frontier settlement where the railroad had not reached. They were another link with a civilized world, an "ox-telegraph" which made life tenable on the plains and which promised better days as goods with all their pertinence to mature living habits flowed onto that sea of prairie which men called the Great Plains.

Opposing that flow throughout the period being looked at here was the Indian, the Plains Indian who con-stituted a frontier and a barrier all his own. For two and one-half centuries, the Plains Indian had withstood the incursions of the Spaniard, English, French, Mexican, and Anglo-American, meanwhile going not altogether peaceably about his business, hunting buffalo, living no-madically, and catching and taming the Spanish horses. But the successive waves of mountain men, Oregon immi-grants, miners, freighters, railroad builders, buffalo hunt-ers, and finally, cattlemen, each after his kind of wealth, contained too many opposing factors to overcome, espe-cially when these factors were augmented by superior numbers, by federal troops, and by greater fire power.

Particularly, the numbers hurt. For numbers had to be fed, and numbers poked and fanned out into the recesses, and numbers beat back the game, and numbers occupied the better land. And numbers spelled destruction for the ridgepole of the Indian's economic dwelling, for numbers spelled the end of the buffalo—the buffalo, Indian companion and mainstay, that at one time ran in herds extending as far toward infinity as a person could see through powerful binoculars, in herds that never faded from view despite days of traveling across the trackless seas of grass, in herds that bellowed and roared like angry waves beating on resisting rocks (always the imagery of the seas and the prairie are inextricable). Colonel Richard Irving Dodge claimed to have traveled 125 miles through a single herd.[14] Numbers took care of all of that.

The Indian of the West depended on the buffalo for food and shelter. But the railroads pushed west, and the buffalo was slaughtered to feed the construction crews. And if that weren't serious enough, there came a near-mania for buffalo robes, so that the hide hunters came thronging in to complete the depletion, with the railroads again aiding with their speedy transportation facilities. In two years, on the southern plains alone, 1,378,359 buffalo hides were shipped to market over three railroads.[15] In vain the Indians pleaded that their game be left alone; in vain the Indians petitioned that their plains be left alone. A tide of men was moving, and the tide's advance was inexorable. Desperately, the Indian fought back, but

[14] H. A. Trexler, "The Buffalo Range of the Northwest," *Mississippi Valley Historical Review*, Vol. VII, No. 4 (March, 1921), 351. Rister, "The Significance of the Destruction of the Buffalo in the Southwest," *Southwestern Historical Quarterly*, Vol. XXXIII, No. 1 (July, 1929), 35–36.

[15] Rister, "The Significance of the Destruction of the Buffalo in the Southwest," *Southwestern Historical Quarterly*, Vol. XXXIII, No. 1 (July, 1929), 42. Buffalo-killing statistics are difficult to swallow nowadays, but the continued emphatic reiterations of individual hunters indicate that there must have been some truth in their figures. Jim McIntire, who is not listed among the most trustworthy (in all seriousness he published an account of his death from black smallpox and of his experiences in the period between death and later resurrection!), claimed that from his camp on the Big Wichita "we could kill all the game we wanted without going one hundred yards from camp" and that their daily take in buffalo hides totaled invariably between fifty and one hundred. McIntire, *Early Days in Texas*, 63–65.

desperation was not sufficient. The tide would surely engulf them, and it did.

As far as the cattleman's frontier is concerned, the Indian barrier may be envisioned as a giant upright triangle, with the Apache occupying the western base, the Comanche dominating the eastern, or Texas, base, and the Sioux at the northern apex. There were other tribes who gave incidental difficulty, but these three are the ones whose names have joined the legends of the cow country.

In dealing with the Indian problem, Texas was more fortunate than the other Western frontier states, for she had maintained a force on her outer fringe since the time of her independence. This force, the famed Texas Rangers, knew Indian habits and Indian methods of warfare, and met Indian onslaughts with such success that it soon became nationally famous, a recognition that has continued down till today, when variegated slot machines cause the Rangers more concern than Comanche war paint. But not even such an efficient force as the Rangers could cope with a thirteen-hundred-mile frontier, nor with hit-and-run raids, especially those by moonlight, from swift, agile ponies which could carry the befeathered marauders miles away before news of the latest outrage could reach the army or the Rangers. And though no Ranger liked to admit it, there lurked the suspicion that the Indian was actually a superior horseman and could take a pony through thick brush that no white man could penetrate.[16]

In the year of the first trail drive into Abilene, the United States signed the Treaty of Medicine Lodge with the Kiowa, Comanche, Cheyenne, Lipan, and Arapahoe tribes guaranteeing Indian withdrawal from the region

[16] Donoho, *Circle–Dot*, 68. Frank Gilbert Roe, *The Indian and the Horse*, 82, says it was agreed that no one could ride like a Comanche.

between the Platte and Arkansas rivers. But the younger tribe members maintained that their older chiefs had been duped by the peace commissioners, and that they were not bound by the treaty. The result was that hostilities soon began to break out all over the plains, the reports mounting in frequency and insistence till finally, in 1871, General William Tecumseh Sherman visited Texas to investigate.

Arriving at Fort Richardson, near Jacksboro, Sherman barely had time to get the red dust removed from his boots (strictly a figure of speech, as Sherman was woefully lacking in military spit-and-polish), when a band of Kiowas and Comanches attacked a government contractor's supply train twenty-two miles away, killing a wagon master and six teamsters. Continuing to Fort Sill, Oklahoma, Sherman asked a group of Kiowas who came to the fort to draw rations whether any of them had participated in the attack on the wagon train and in the mutilation which followed it.

To Sherman's complete consternation, one chief, Satanta, boasted that he had led the raid. There followed five minutes of tenseness (which General Sherman, according to Paul Wellman, met with "monolithic coolness") in which both Indians and white soldiers leveled guns at each other. But in the end, Satanta and two of his associates, Satank and Big Tree, surrendered to arrest. Shortly Satanta and Big Tree were sent to a term in the Texas state prison, while Satank committed suicide by pretending an escape attempt, thereby drawing seven bullets from the guards. Such arrests, however, failed to stop Indian depredations. By 1875, though, the Indians above and below the Red River had largely been subdued, and after another five years, the Mescalero Apaches and other irreconcilable tribes which made periodic forays into Texas from New Mexico bases also decided that peace was preferable to elimination. From 1880 onward, Texas could pursue its cattle running without much fear of Indian depredations.[17]

Arizona was less fortunate. Apache atrocities there excited such vengeful feelings among the whites that they perpetrated retaliatory cruelties even on friendly tribes. Arizona soon reached a stage in which no one could live at peace, red or white. The Apache wars reached a climax in the 1880's, when Geronimo, that thin-lipped, square-cut, hard-eyed, savagely cruel hater of all white men, threatened to make southern Arizona and northern Mexico his personal kingdom. In one six months' period, Geronimo's raiders officially killed eighty-five soldiers, settlers, and reservation Indians in American territory, besides an uncounted number below the Mexican border, while losing only six warriors themselves. The best Indian fighters in the army went after the Apaches, with uniform failure. Finally, General Nelson A. Miles was given the assignment. Using twenty-five detachments, he combed the country on both sides of the border. The pursuit was relentless, and the result foreseeable. Now very definitely the hunted, Geronimo turned to needless terror, killing, among others, between five and six hundred Sonorans during his campaign to escape capture. Finally, in September, 1886, at Skeleton Canyon, Geronimo, after preliminary consultations, surrendered, winding up eventually at Fort Sill, where he was to live almost another quarter-century.[18] Like other areas, Arizona's day as an Indian frontier had come to a peaceful, if not altogether

[17] Rister, *Southwestern Frontier*, 74–75, 107, 130, 147 ff., 180, 216. Wellman, *Glory, God and Gold*, 348–49. Rupert Norval Richardson, *The Comanche Barrier to South Plains Settlement*, 341–45.
[18] Dale, *The Indians of the Southwest*, 95 ff. Wellman, *Glory, God and Gold*, 360–67.

glorious, end, leaving cowboys free to concentrate their fire on sheepherders and nesters. Meanwhile, the fiction and movie writers let their imaginations run riot without too much fear of exaggeration, their accounts of Indian-cowboy clashes being checked only by good taste, for the far Southwest was truly a malevolent ground.

In the Indian Territory, that huge tract between Texas and Kansas set aside strictly for the red man, the Indian was more of a nuisance than a problem, as far as the Anglo-American was concerned. Although white entrance into Indian Territory was supposed to be strictly regu-lated, the barrier failed to restrict the long drives and the range cattle business between the Red River and the Kan-sas border. The grass in Oklahoma was just as fattening as the grass in Texas, and this route was one or two hundred miles nearer the market, so the cattle were driven in. In-dians might collect a toll for each trail herd passing through their area, but payment was cheap tribute for the benefit derived farther on. Besides, the government was willing to lease certain range areas.[19] Oklahoma was cat-tleman's country a good dozen years before it was offi-cially white man's country.

The northern apex of the triangle is a Sioux story with the same general theme as that of the Comanche and Apache countries, a story of the Indian's last-ditch stand against the white invasion of his hunting country. After the range cattle industry spread rather quickly into south-ern Wyoming, its expansion tended to stall. The country beyond the North Platte and the Sweetwater, and be-tween the Big Horn Mountains and the Missouri River was impenetrable, for it was either Indian reservation or hunting ground. An attempt in the 1860's to connect Mon-tana with the East by the Bozeman Trail had been fought

[19] Dale, *The Range Cattle Industry*, 135–38.

off by the Sioux under Red Cloud. Now the government determined to make another effort.

The first attempt was to persuade the Indians to open the Black Hills. That failed. The government then announced that any miner could go into northern Indian land who had sufficient intrepidity or foolhardiness. The Sioux responded with open revolt, with results that have added enormous color to our Western lore. (The color, incidentally, is primarily red.) In the process of subduing the Sioux, General Custer made himself immortal in the best historical tradition by rash tactics which resulted in the total destruction of his force (Why is it that in military folklore defeats are so much more glorious than victories —Custer's Little Big Horn, the Alamo, Dunkirk, Gettysburg?). Custer won, of course, for his defeat in the year the United States was celebrating its centennial in Philadelphia led to a demand that such indignities at the hands of an "inferior" people be halted at once. Clearing the northern plains of the Indian barrier became only a matter of time. The buffalo was gone; the Indian wouldn't be far behind.

Not a single frontier process of the Great Plains but had its era of high adventure and romance. And not a single frontier process but touched the cowboy, if not actually, at least in a fusion induced by time and distance. The Oregon immigrant, the stagecoach driver, the bullwhacker, the Western soldier, the railroad builder, and the Indian—each has his role in the enactment of the cowboy epic, all are a part of the web of myth which surrounds the one figure, the cowboy, who somehow emerged as the leading actor in an age that was thought of as heroic even while it was still in existence, an age whose luster time has failed to diminish.

9. The Literature
Before 1900

A CENTURY and a quarter ago, a Yankee whale-ship, the *Essex*, was rammed by a sperm whale with such force that her bow was stove in and she was swallowed by the Pacific Ocean within ten minutes. Nearly another quarter of a century went by before the *Essex* got her chronicler, Herman Melville, who made her sinking the climax of *Moby Dick*, his classic of whaling.

The range cattle industry and its legendary worker, the cowboy, were not so fortunate. The frontier cowboy closed shop about 1890. A quarter of a century went by, but the complete chronicler had not appeared to immortalize

140

the cowboy in literature. Now nearly three quarters of a century have passed, and still we await his appearance. Is the cowboy not so worthy a subject as the whaler? We rather think he is, but still we await the great American novel to tell us so.

In the opening salvo of this study, some statistics were given regarding the cowboy story. If you recall, one stated that nearly one thousand titles were listed in *Book Review Digest*. In addition, the short stories featuring the cowboy are so numerous that to try to capture them in statistics would be like trying to count red ants on the prairie. The point is that there has been a mass of cowboy literature, and that out of that literature have come some good, if not great, works, some stories that have captured the cowboy with fidelity, some stories that have captured him with imagination, and even some that have combined these two qualities.

There is another point. To try to blanket the field of cowboy fiction would be to smother you beneath that blanket. *Moby Dick* appeared within a quarter of a century after the *Essex* sank. Suppose then we largely confine ourselves to the first quarter of a century following the closing of the range in examining the story of the cowboy as told by the purveyors of commercialized imagination. Except to spill over for an occasional comparison, this chapter will concentrate on a critical interpretation and evaluation of cowboy fiction from 1890 to 1915, treating such literature, so-called and legitimate, as a distinct literary genre, making no attempt to get outside the cowboy genre to compare *The Log of a Cowboy* with *Moby Dick*, or *Wolfville* with *Huckleberry Finn*.

This time delimitation has validity, for the period between 1890 and 1915 is a focal point for cowboy fiction. What appeared before 1890 either had no literary merit or was just plain sub-literary. The range fiction appearing since 1915 parallels in pattern and artistic merit the literature within our quarter-century, the only differences being a slight shift in market taste, a polishing of style, and a flirtation with Freud.

Historically, the basis for ranch literature existed from the time the Anglo-Americans first settled in Texas, and the descendants of the *rancheros* in California and the *pastores* in New Mexico will insist that the basis should be placed further back than Texas. Cowboy stories had made an appearance, if not exactly created a vogue, well before the Civil War. And by the time the range closed down, the cowboy myth was already acknowledged. Our Western story of 1890–1915 then actually created no myth but enlarged and enhanced the color and the romance of the legend. When Owen Wister, toward whom most sombreros are waved when men talk of the beginnings of cowboy fiction, wrote *Lin McLean* in 1898, he was aware that he was not creating a legend, but that he was working with a lore which had already become a part of American folk life. And through the decades, it has been those writers—or panderers, as the more self-consciously artistic might say—who were aware of the myth and tried to transmit and prolong it who have been most successful. Eugene Manlove Rhodes wrote from atop a literary mesa as compared with Zane Grey in his valley wasteland. But Grey knew that the public's interest lay not in the cowboy as he actually was, but as the American folk hero his public wanted him to be. Rhodes knew what the cowboy actually was, and wrote accordingly. Fifty people have read Grey for one who has read Rhodes, and that includes the reading cowboy.

Actually, "ranch fiction" preceded "cowboy stories" along the literary trail, the cowboy emerging only after he began to take on folk qualities. In the 1850's, Charles W. Webber came out with his collection of *Tales of the Southern Border*, a blend of romanticism and naturalism which alternately sentimentalizes over Texas frontier life and criticizes the crudities and brutalities of that same life. Although Webber's stories are not cowboy stories in the later sense, the cowboy appears on occasion, remarkably akin to his descendant a couple of decades later. For example, in one of the stories set on a *ranchero,* the host, commenting on the abundance promised by a generous Nature, adds that "the ingenuity of Colt has guaranteed us, in his revolvers, a secure possession" of this abundance. "I can only control the savage herd about me by the terror which the constant presence of this . . . really formidable weapon inspires," he observes.[1] The Colt reappears a few years later in Theodore Winthrop's *John Brent*, laid among roping and horsebreaking *vaqueros* on a California *ranchero.* Talking about riding a wild horse leads one character to remark: "Ef you ever ride or back that curwolyow, I'll eat a six-shooter, loaded and capped."[2]

In each decade up to 1890, the ranch story could be traced, but usually the story would be the same. Ranch life is depicted with some care; the cowboy is a character but seldom a leading one. He is around, but he is in the shadows. *Lippincott's Magazine* carried a story in 1880 entitled "Sargent's Rodeo," which had a lot to say about the roundup, roping, and branding of cattle, but comparatively little about the cowboy.[3] Even in the early 1890's, Mary Hallock Foote, whom Wister mentions with admira-

---

[1] *Tales of the Southern Border*, 242.

[2] *John Brent*, 28.

[3] F. M. Osbourne, "Sargent's Rodeo," *Lippincott's Magazine*, Vol. XXV (January, 1880), 9 ff. A year later in *Lippincott's* February issue appeared " 'The Kid': A Chapter in Wyoming," in which several references are made to the "Cow-boy" and the "cow-puncher."

tion in his *Members of the Family*, was able to write stories of ranch life with only casual mention of the cowboy and range rider.[4]

Stories and novels in which the cowboy played a reasonably major role did begin to appear within a dozen years after the first longhorns were trailed into Abilene. Thomas Pilgrim, who wrote under the pseudonym of Arthur Morecamp, wrote perhaps the first strictly cowboy fiction. His first novel, *Live Boys; or Charley and Nasho in Texas*, is based on the adventures of a Texas trail drive into Kansas. Written for boys, it treats both preparation for the drive and the adventures of the drive itself.

Pilgrim's second novel appeared a year later in 1880. In several respects, *Live Boys in the Black Hills* is more important than the earlier work, for it includes descriptions of the trail, a Kansas cowtown, and Deadwood, Dakota Territory, the end of the trail. Most of the standard Western items are present—the cattle trail, the mining frontier, buffalo, Indians, dance hall brawls, and blazing six-guns. Calamity Jane enters—"on the street on horseback, riding straddle, drunk as a fool, and cutting up like a greaser on a spree."[5] The cowboy is here, but he is hardly a hero, that role being reserved for the two "Live Boys."

Scribner's tried an adult approach, or more precisely, an approach for adult readers, in its March, 1880, issue with a story entitled "Over Sunday at New Sharon," depicting a Sunday in Dodge City. Here, while Dodge City was wallowing in its lusty glory, the cowboy definitely occupies a position upstage:

[4] "A Touch of the Sun," *Century Magazine,* Vol. LIX, No. 3 (January, 1900), is a good example of Miss Foote at her serious Western best. Owen Wister, *Members of the Family,* 15.
[5] Arthur Morecamp, *Live Boys in the Black Hills,* 293.

Everywhere, the cow-boys made themselves manifest, clad now in the soiled and dingy jeans of the trail, and then in a suit of many buttoned corduroy, and again in affluence of broadcloth, silk hat, gloves, cane, and sometimes a clerical white neck tie. And everywhere, also, stared and shone the Lone Star of Texas —for the cow-boy, wherever he may wander, and however he may change, never forgets to be a Texan, and never spends his money or lends his presence to a concern that does not in some way recognize the emblem of his native state.[6]

These stories have no significance, unless it is in their timing. But they do drive home the point that the cowboy was in the process of being discovered while the range was still open, and that the cowboy, like America awaiting on Isabella, needed only a sponsor to make his presence felt throughout the nation.

The sponsor appeared when the publishing house of Beadle and Adams took the cowboy under its fictional wing and promoted widespread acceptance in an incredibly brief time. The "Wild West" had been in the Beadle and Adams catalogs for a quarter-century before the cowboy began to emerge as a leading fictional character, but when he did come out of the wings in the 1880's, Beadle and Adams had a ready-made reading audience of considerable proportions palpitating for any hero bearing the Beadle and Adams imprint.

Until the cowboy, the dime novel had exploited such famous frontier personalities as Kit Carson, Calamity Jane, and Deadwood Dick, the innocuous Richard Clark, in an ever wider separation between fact and fiction. Buffalo Bill was regularly turning out autobiographical experiences, most of them written by a soldier of fortune named

[6] *Scribner's Monthly*, Vol. XIX, No. 5 (March, 1880), 771.

Prentiss Ingraham, who in his way was as fabulous as Cody. Ingraham, who had fought with Juarez, in Austria, Crete, Egypt, Cuba, and with Buffalo Bill, wrote nearly a thousand novels himself, all in longhand, sometimes at virtually one sitting—one took him all of a day and a half.[7] You can disparage the quality, but the quantity is truly prodigious. Even the more modest output of Edward L. Wheeler, the creator of the Deadwood Dick series, is startling by most modern comparisons. Wheeler, incidentally, is interesting as a type of cowboy writer. He looked like a theologian, greeted all strangers as "pard," never traveled west of Illinois, spent most of his life in Pennsylvania, and was not incapable of placing Cheyenne east of the Black Hills of South Dakota or of other fantastic geographical errors. And he did all of this in a life that lasted a mere thirty years.[8]

To continue this divergence from fact, when the range rider with his fast draw and his Apache-slaying proclivities became a standard hero, proved no feat at all. But the cowboy was doomed to a short life as a strictly dime-novel hero, for writers of a somewhat higher caste, such as Wister, were only a decade or so away. By 1907, one critic was already certain that "the cowboy as a picturesque feature of the Western landscape has passed out and the dime novel will know him no more."[9] But in 1955, the pulp magazine and the pocket book carry on in the dime-novel tradition, and today it is the dime novel that is gone, not the dime-novel cowboy.

Two of the more recent looks at the cowboy and Beadle and Adams are the monumental bibliography, *The House of Beadle and Adams,* by Albert Johannsen, and the pro-

[7] Johannsen, *House of Beadle and Adams,* II, 155–60.
[8] *Ibid.,* II, 293–98.
[9] Charles M. Harvey, "The Dime Novel in American Life," *Atlantic Monthly,* Vol. C (July, 1907), 44.

vocative article in *Studies in English* by Warren French, who suggests that only four of the firm's staff wrote a sufficient number of novels to provide a body of work in which the cowboy assumed discernible characteristics. Each of the writers tackled the cowboy from a different point of view, French says. Joseph Badger, Jr., one of the earliest, wrote with restraint, humor, and some realism. Captain Frederick Whittaker, an ex-Union army officer, on the other hand, was decidedly hostile. He saw the cowboy as a reversion to primitive man—lawless and uncultured, which may have been realistic, except that he didn't paint the cowboy against a backdrop of a sometimes lawless and uncultured frontier. The third writer, Prentiss Ingraham, already met as a fictional chronicler of Buffalo Bill, draped his novels around the frame of Buck Taylor, a cowboy in Cody's Wild West show. French credits William G. Patten, the fourth of the Beadle and Adams cowboy quartet, as the novelist who lifted the cowboy from a subordinate to a central figure in the Western literary genre. Patten's men were men of action, risking their necks in turning stampedes and resisting theft in chasing rustlers. They were men of honor and integrity, nature's noblemen.[10]

Beadle and Adams shared the later preoccupation with Texas as a subject for exaggerated fiction. A quick rundown of the firm's titles beginning with the word "Texas" reveals a total of forty-one, and the number which have "Texas" farther along in the title or which are wrapped around Texas topics must be tremendous. Whether it was the influence of the Texas cowboy is unknown, but the name Texas apparently carried a connotation of lawlessness, as indicated by such titles as *Terrible Texans, Terror Tom of Texas,* and *Terrible Six from Texas.* We must con-

[10] Warren French, "The Cowboy in the Dime Novel," *Studies in English,* Vol. XXX (1951), 219 ff.

fess, though, that to us the most intriguing title in the list may have nothing to do with cowboys whatsoever. When we spotted *Red-Light Ralph's Resolve,* we were sorely tempted to drop this study and go on a search for a copy.[11]

Seriously again, the Beadle and Adams stable, working in the aggregate, hit the cowboy from at least four different angles, as French suggests. And as far as paternity is concerned, the nickel and dime publishers can claim that 1955's fictional cowboy child is theirs by reason of a rough resemblance.

Whatever may be due the early ranch stories or the novels of Beadle and Adams, Owen Wister is the writer who made the American cowboy palatable to Eastern readers and therefore worthy of recognition by the literary critics. Philadelphia-born, Harvard-educated (*summa cum laude* in music, Class of '82), Wister made a trip to the West in 1882, was impressed, and returned to Wyoming in 1891 for health and big game, both of which were available in quantity. In that same year, he sold his first story to *Harper's.*[12]

From the first, Wister seems to have been aware that in the cowboy he was dealing with a distinct class of frontiersman, and Lin McLean, his first cowboy creation, is the Virginian a little less surely etched. Look at this description:

He was a complete specimen of his lively and peculiar class. Cow-punchers are not a race. . . . They gallop over the face of the empty earth for a little while, and those whom rheumatism or gunpowder does not overtake, are blotted out by the course of the empire, leaving no trace behind.[13]

[11] Johannsen, *House of Beadle and Adams,* II, 394, 405.
[12] Unless otherwise cited, biographical information in this chapter and in the next is from Stanley J. Kuntz and Howard Haycraft (eds.), *Twentieth Century Authors.*
[13] Wister, "How Lin McLean Went East," *Harper's New Monthly Magazine,* Vol. LXXXVI, No. DXI, (December, 1892), 135.

The story is told simply. Lin McLean, a robust young bachelor, has left the range with his wages to visit his brother, a sophisticated Bostonian. Humorously, Wister relates McLean's sampling of a sermon, a mild flirtation, a poker game in which he is cleaned, a gold prospect, and, of course, the trip East, where he learns that he no longer fits into Boston society and returns happily to the West.

Six years later, the *Harper's* story reappeared as the first chapter of a full-length, if somewhat episodic, novel titled *Lin McLean*. As before, the treatment is lighthearted and based on the sometimes uncouth and boisterous joking of the frontiersmen. McLean, incidentally, wears his six-shooter strapped low on his right leg, which in a moment of stress might make him a most likely candidate to shoot himself. The novel has an adumbrative interest, for both the Virginian and Molly Wood, the Bear Creek school mistress, appear. As might be suspected, the Virginian is already nobler than Lin McLean. Already too, Wister is getting sentimental about the cowboy, as most Western writers invariably do. McLean, he says on the very first page, "lived in the old days, the happy days, when Wyoming was a Territory with a future instead of a state with a past." Later McLean observes: "Someday we punchers won't be here. The living will be scattered, and the dead—well, they'll be all right. Have yu' studied the wire fence? It's spreading to catch us like nets do the salmon in the Columbia River." [14] To a nation that knows little of Arthur and nothing at all of Roland or Amadis, the legends of Lin McLean strike responsive ears which detect here a vanishing type.

In 1900, *The Jimmyjohn Boss*, another Wister collection, appeared. It is not convincing, though one sketch, "Hank's Woman," a psychological study of Williomene, an Austrian maid who marries Hank after being dismissed as

[14] Wister, *Lin McLean*, 1, 160.

an incompetent domestic, possesses genuine merit. Williomene comes to despise Hank, and the story ends in murder and suicide.

Meanwhile, other writers of some quality, of whom two at least should be mentioned, were being attracted by Western possibilities. Indeed, one of them, Alfred Henry Lewis, was considered ahead of Wister as the century made its turn. Lewis, born in Cleveland in 1859, had been city attorney of Cleveland at twenty-one. Later he had spent time in Arizona and New Mexico and had practiced law in Kansas City, after which he became a successful newspaper man.

Lewis' *Wolfville*, published in 1897, became an immediate commercial success. Written with serious intent and from personal observations in Tombstone and Charleston, Arizona, it was serious only in execution, for it is a humorous burlesque of frontier personalities. There is no malice, nor any attempt at satire in the Mark Twain sense—just broad, seasoned, gaudy fun and exaggeration at the hands of the cowboy, miner, sheriff, outlaw, and dance hall girls. Bret Harte's influence is clearly discernible, but unlike Harte, Lewis does not create diamonds in the rough. His Wolfville folks are whatever they are, and just sometimes are their motives good. The sentimental and picaresque are not compatible in *Wolfville*.

Wolfville is also a collection held together by the narrator, the Old Cattleman. It starts on a high note with a grand spoof of a gambler's funeral, which represents Wolfville's opportunity to lord it over rival Red Dog. Doc Peets is the master of ceremonies and he knows how to go about getting ready:

"It's the chance of our life," says Doc Peets, "an' we plays it. Thar's nothin' too rich for our blood, an' these obsequies is goin' to be spread-eagle, you bet! We'll show Red Dog an' similar villages they ain't sign-camps compared with Wolf-ville." [15]

Doc demands that the hole be dug at least a mile from camp, for to have a successful funeral, "you needs distance." Further, he tells the preacher, "We wants nothin' but good words. Don't mind about the trooth." [16] When finally the gambler is buried, the folk of Wolfville honor him with a head board:

JaCK KinG
LIfE AiN'T
in
Holding a Good Hand
But
In Playing a Pore Hand
Well.[17]

Lewis knew how to handle the tall tale. Texas Thompson and Old Jim Bridger spent a Thanksgiving in the Great Salt Lake Valley. Snow fell on top of snow, six feet deep, bogging down twenty thousand buffaloes. Texas Thompson and Bridger cut the throat of each animal, left them till the spring thaw, and then rolled them into the Salt Lake, where the briny water promptly pickled them. Now Texas Thompson and Bridger returned from trapping each year by way of the Great Salt Lake, fished out however many buffaloes they wanted, and gorged themselves.[18]

Such stories brought an immediately enthusiastic audience, too enthusiastic perhaps for Lewis' modest talents. In 1902, he tried to enlarge his reputation with *Wolfville*

[15] Alfred Henry Lewis, *Wolfville*, 2.
[16] *Ibid.*, 3.
[17] *Ibid.*, 8.
[18] *Ibid.*, 259–60.

Days and again with *Wolfville Nights,* six years later he brought out *Wolfville Folks,* and in 1913 he made a final appearance with *Faro Nell.* In between these major works, numerous stories appeared in popular magazines. They all provided a good living, but didn't avoid the problem of working a good idea to death with sheer repetition. Nowadays, unfairly really, Lewis is passed over casually, but at the turn of the century he was considered a front-rank practitioner operating only a plane below Harte and Twain, but operating from such a wide plane that his advertising of Western frontier humor represented a contribution of continuing significance.

One of the best Western novels in the nineties appeared two years before *Wolfville* was published. Arthur Paterson's *A Son of the Plains* pictures the sheepmen-cattlemen war and works out a story of rather high literary quality, despite such stock situations as the stagecoach robbery and the pitched battle between the cattleman and the sheepman. In his book, Paterson treats the range rider as a dominant hero type, and he does it with attention to authenticity.

At the turn of the century, another first-novel appeared which acts as a transition from the nineteenth to the twentieth century concept of cowboy fiction. Titled appropriately *The Girl at the Halfway House,* it represents the position or attitude halfway between the feeling toward a cowboy hero in the 1890's and the popular, if not completely artistic, realization of that hero in the decade and a half ahead. When it appeared, it attracted little attention, and it has scarcely been mentioned since, but it is unquestionably the best of the Western novels turned out by its later famous author, Emerson Hough.

Hough knew his West, veer though he might from the historical straight and narrow along his fictional path.

Born in Newton, Iowa, of a pioneer Iowa family, he taught school before winding up with a law degree from the University of Iowa and locating in a tiny frontier town between the Pecos and Rio Grande in New Mexico. It was a wild, rough place, "half cow-town and half mining camp," and the young attorney had the discernment to realize that he was witnessing a passing historical pageant which in his mind took the form of plots and stories.[19] A contributor of short stories to magazines while still in college, he now began to record in earnest. By 1897, he had brought out his nonfictional *The Story of the Cowboy*, which nearly sixty years later still endures as a popular standard. However, his most celebrated works, *North of 36* and *The Covered Wagon*, belong to the 1920's, when Hough had reached his mid-sixties.

The Girl at the Halfway House tells the story of the wasteful, riotous days of the cattle drives, and of the suffering, starving, killing, and raw life associated with a virile and daring frontier. Underlying the story runs the theme of man's enthusiastic expression of his atavistic nature, which he buries under a veneer sometimes thin, sometimes comfortably thick.

The novel is divided into four major parts. It begins with a closing battle in the Civil War in which Captain Edward Franklin, a Union officer of the engineers, watches a Southern girl searching the battlefield for her dead lover. Later they meet in Ellisville, a Kansas depot teeming with Texas longhorns, and—and this is desiccating a tender romance with brevity—they fall in love. Ellisville could be Abilene, Dodge City, or any railroad town in between.

The second part of the novel disposes of the buffalo.

[19] Pauline Graham, "Novelist of the Unsung," *The Palimpsest*, Vol. XI, No. 2 (February, 1930), 69.

Franklin watched the hide hunters, going out, coming in, "unloading their cargoes of bleached bones at the side of the railroad track," the heap of bones growing "vast, white, ghastly, formidable, higher than a house, more than a bowshot long." [20]

In its third part, *The Girl at the Halfway House* gets around to the story of interest to us—the cattlemen's frontier. Here Hough, who is not above writing dated prose, reaches vivid heights that deserve to be quoted for their continuing interest. He saw the trail herds as follows:

There came on the great herds of gaunt, broad-horned cattle, footsore and slow and weary with their march of more than a thousand miles. These vast herds deployed in turn about the town of Ellisville, the Mecca for which they had made this unprecedented pilgrimage. They trampled down every incipient field, and spread abroad over all the grazing lands. . . . Herd after herd passed still farther north, past Ellisville, going on wearily another thousand miles, to found the Ellisvilles of the upper range. [21]

The eddying of a booming frontier town like Ellisville is particularly well handled. Here is one description:

The town became a loadstone for the restless population ever crowding out upon the uttermost frontier. The men from the farther East dropped their waistcoats and their narrow hats at Ellisville. All the world went under wide felt and bore a jingling spur. Every man was armed. The pitch of life was high. It was worth death to live a year in such a land. [22]

Hough was aware of the importance that such a frontier town would eventually have on American literature:

[20] Hough, *The Girl at the Halfway House*, 70.
[21] *Ibid.*, 168.
[22] *Ibid.*, 168–69.

Over all the world, unaided by a sensational press, and as yet without even that non-resident literature which was later to discover the Ellisvilles after the Ellisvilles were gone, there spread the fame of Ellisville the Red, the lustful, the unspeakable. Here was a riot of animal intensity of life, a mutiny of physical man, the last outbreak of innate savagery of primitive man against the day of shackles and subjugation. The men of that rude day lived vehemently. They died, they escaped. The earth is trampled over their bold hearts, and they have gone back into the earth, the air, the sky, and the wild flowers.[23]

Hough gives a description of the cowboy that could have come from any 1955 movie script. It is colorful, it is exaggerated, and it is what the public wants to hear: "Wild men from the range," he wrote, "rode their horses up the steps and into the bar-room, demanding to be served as they sat in their saddle, as gentlemen should." The town marshal was due his share of attention—"a heavily built man, sandy-haired, red-moustached, and solid," with bow legs and thick fingers that belied their deftness, a man "careful in his shooting, because he is careless of being shot," a man who contended "(while he was alive) that a man with one gun was as good as a man with two." [24] Naturally the marshal winds up in a gun duel with the town's badman and gun artist.

If Hough is guilty of coloring his historical materials, it must also be admitted that his spirit is more genuine than in the ordinary range novel. Thus he describes the passing day of the cattleman:

Far as the eye could reach, the long and dusty roadway of the cows lay silent, with its dust unstirred. Far, very far off there was approaching a little band of strange, small, bleating, wooly creatures, to whose driver, Mother Daly refused bed

[23] *Ibid.*, 170.
[24] *Ibid.*, 234–36.

and board. The cattle chutes were silent, the corral empty. . . . Up and down the trail, east and west of the trail, all was quiet, bare and desolate. . . . The cowman, the railroad man, and the gambling man had gone, leaving behind them the wide and well-perforated Cottage, the graveyard with its double street. . . .[25]

The concluding portion of the novel is told through the eyes of the farmer who enters the area with his family and his plow, supplanting the old frontier order. There are faults in *The Girl at the Halfway House,* but most of them are not our concern here. What does concern us is that in *Halfway House* Hough has written a turn-of-the-century novel that tries to take its West seriously and that foreshadows the cowboy-Western fiction of the years ahead. Only two years ahead lay Wister's *The Virginian,* the generally acknowledged starting point for the cowboy as he has developed in American literature. *The Girl at the Halfway House* makes a proper steppingstone for *The Virginian.*

And so the twentieth century arrived, with the fictional cowboy having behind him an apprenticeship of a quarter of a century. Already his period of range and trail were being decked out in the colors of the myth and legend makers. And they could lead the reading public, who would be mostly in the East, in almost any direction they chose, for the Eastern readers had no actual knowledge of what the West was like, or of what it should be like; but they had imagination, and the writers were learning how to exploit that imagination.

But even at the turn of the century, there were few, if any, signs that the American cowboy would one day command the reading interest of a large segment of the Amer-

[25] *Ibid.,* 288–89.

ican reading public. In 1900, no one could know that a dominant American folk hero would come forth in less than two year's time, a folk hero who would still be around nearly six decades later. The seeds had been planted—actually, they had only been scattered; but they were taking root, and when men like Wister and Hough began to fertilize and nurture those seeds in the years ahead, a tremendous harvest of cowboy fiction was going to be ready.

10. The Literature
After 1900

THE Western range novel came of age when, after an apprenticeship of more than ten years of writing Western fiction, Owen Wister presented the American public with *The Virginian* to elevate cowboy fiction to a distinct category. Although *The Virginian* is not a representative novel of the cattlemen's frontier, nor the Virginian a fair representation of the cowboy, both the novel and its hero have won enduring acceptance in American literature. For most long-time readers of the Western story, the Virginian has become the final apotheosis of the range rider.

One reason that Wister's *Virginian* has withstood the

158

test of time and has won partial acclaim by the literary critic lies in the fact that Wister wrote of a West "that was" —a reasonably straightforward, artistic treatment of materials based on credible Western motifs and themes. Faults abound. You may question the advisability of letting Molly Wood ride unescorted on the range, or of Wister's injecting philosophical justifications of his work when no justifications are necessary, or of comparing western and southern lynching. Furthermore, it takes no great perception to see that Wister borrows readily from Bret Harte and Mark Twain in spirit, if not in actual plot. The story of Shorty, the dupe of Trampas, and his lamentable end echoes the sentimental picaresque treatment of Harte. The story of Emily the hen is out of phase with the spirit of *The Virginian*, and sounds more like the kind of tale Twain would tell with gusto.

Wister labored to make the novel acceptable to an Eastern audience, and as far as that goes, to himself. Schoolmistress Molly Wood is the link connecting the uneducated Virginian and the unconfined West with the Eastern audience. Wister strove to make the Virginian, obviously a cultural inferior, worthy of Molly, and at the same time to show the basically heroic qualities of his character. The Virginian is a man of honesty and virility, healthy, deeply loving, strong, shrewd, fun-loving and gentle—containing all the personal qualities inherent in the heroes of any race or nation, from daring in battle to gallantry in love, and always with tremendous reserve. He has everything except the advantage of breeding, which can be overcome by the love and example of a good woman.

The choice of a Virginian was a happy one, for those graceful blue ridges and pleasant pastures and soft voices are associated with style and knowing horsemanship and worldly compatibility. If he had been a Texan, there would have been no grace, only *gaucherie*. He would have been a wild child of the wilderness, unconversant with literature, and unteachable. He would have been half-outlaw, and the only reason he wouldn't have been all outlaw would have been because he had never been properly provoked. But he might have been slightly more true to the spirit of the time.

But all Texas outlooks aside, the Virginian is a proper hero, worthy of taking his place alongside the other heroes in the cowboy's fictional hall of fame. Look at him,

lounging there at ease against the wall . . . a slim young giant, more beautiful than pictures. His broad, soft hat was pushed back; a loose-knotted, dull-scarlet handkerchief sagged from his throat; and one casual thumb was hooked in the cartridge belt that slanted across his hips. He had plainly come many miles from somewhere across the vast horizon, as the dust upon him showed.[1]

To teach such a man, Molly Wood makes an appropriate companion. If, in the beginning, she lacks the spirit of aboriginal simplicity that would lead her to accept the action of the vigilante committee or the Virginian's dueling on the eve of his wedding, she learns about the West; and as she learns, she shows an essentially fine-grained but tough stock that is fit to be grafted onto this southern strain. Certainly *The Virginian,* whatever its faults, whatever its banalities, is no common book. Despite sporadic carping from the critics, it has led all competitors for more than fifty years.

In the same year as *The Virginian,* another book appeared that so closely resembled it in plot that the two authors of the two books could have been accused of collab-

[1] Wister, *The Virginian,* 4.

oration. Frances McElrath's *The Rustler, A Tale of Love and War in Wyoming* had the misfortune to appear almost simultaneously with *The Virginian* and to be not so good a book. The authoress had spent most of her life on Western ranches and at army posts and knew her West firsthand. She wrote a book that was crude, melodramatic, and over-sentimental, but a book with a certain emotive vitality. It was the sort of novel of which critics say that the author has talent and promise. With Miss McElrath, the promise was never fulfilled. Her cowboy is a Texan, intelligent but as crude as only fictional—and sometimes mortal—Texans can be. He turns rustler when an Eastern girl of breeding plays with his love, and from that point on the story runs parallel to the Johnson County War. The novel was quickly forgotten, but is worth a passing glance here because Miss McElrath wrote a pioneer Western cowboy novel which showed a fine feeling for the forces at work on the cattleman's frontier.

Although *The Virginian* may have captured the public's fancy as the all-time cowboy classic, the critics almost unanimously salute another novel when the all-time honors are being declared. That book is Andy Adams' *The Log of a Cowboy*, a book praised by about as many critics and historians of the West as by general readers, but a book that seems destined to endure. Here is what J. Frank Dobie says of the novel:

If all literature on whales and whalers were destroyed with the exception of *Moby Dick,* we could still get from that novel a conception of whaling. Likewise, if all of the literature pertaining to trailing were destroyed, we could still get a conception of trailing cattle from Andy Adams.[2]

[2] Frank V. Dearing (ed.), *The Best Novels and Stories of Eugene Manlove Rhodes,* xii–xiii.

Dobie must believe in Andy Adams, for twenty-three years before he made the foregoing statement, he wrote that "*The Log of a Cowboy* is the best book that has ever been written . . . and . . . —that ever can be written of cowboy life." [3]

Dobie's enthusiasm is buttressed by Walter Prescott Webb, who can never be accused of being in automatic agreement with his distinguished fellow-critic of the Western scene. Says Webb:

Hitherto there has been written but one novel of the cattle kingdom that is destined to become a classic—*The Log of a Cowboy*, by Andy Adams; yet in spite of its simple beauty of style, its pellucid clarity, and its verisimilitude, this book first published in 1903, has escaped recognition until recently. The historians, the anthologists, and the literary critics have failed to recognize it as worthy of note in their bibliographies, perhaps because they lack the basis of judgment. [4]

Acclaim has been handed *The Log of a Cowboy* for its faithful and minute recording of a trail drive of longhorns from the Rio Grande to the Blackfoot agency in Montana. Throughout, accuracy and a fidelity to the true West dominate Adams' account. The following quotation is but one example of how Adams, even though his hero "took to the range as a preacher's son takes to vice," refused to let himself be persuaded to jazz the facts to suit the imagination. [5] The sensational press and the romantic Western fiction had made Dodge City, with its intersections of east–west transcontinental trails, Western cattle trail, and Atchison, Topeka, and Santa Fe, a sort of bloody angle of the plains. Adams stuck to the truth:

[3] Dobie, "Andy Adams, Cowboy Chronicler," *Southwest Review,* Vol. XI, No. 2 (January, 1926), 93.

[4] *The Great Plains,* 462.

[5] Adams, *The Log of a Cowboy,* 7.

"I've been in Dodge every summer since '77," said the old cowman, "and I can give you boys some points. Dodge is one town where the average bad man of the West not only finds his equal, but finds himself badly handicapped. The buffalo hunters and range men have protested against the iron rule of Dodge's peace officers, and nearly every protest has cost a life. Don't ever get the impression that you can ride your horses into a saloon, or shoot out the lights in Dodge; it may go somewhere else, but it don't go there. So I warn you to behave yourselves. You can wear your six-shooters into town, but you'd better leave them at the first place you stop. . . . Most cowboys think it's an infringement on their rights to give up shooting in town, and if it is, it stands, for your six-shooters are no match for Winchesters and buckshot; and Dodge's officers are as game a set of men as ever faced danger." [6]

Although Adams was by no means a one-shot author, none of his subsequent books quite came up to *The Log of a Cowboy*. In 1904, the year after *The Log*, Adams wrote *A Texas Matchmaker*, written around the person of a powerful Texas rancher who wants to match his *vaqueros* and Mexican maidens. In this book, Adams seems to have left his natural artistic milieu, and he fumbles. Two years later he tried another trail book, *The Outlet*, which is adequate but no more than that.

With *Reed Anthony, Cowman*, Adams attempted a thinly veiled biography of Charles Goodnight, the Texas Panhandle cattle king. This effort resulted in at least a minor classic, though Adams was given scant applause for it. But it is as good an account of the rising fortunes of a Texas rancher as is likely to be encountered, told as usual with Adams' sincere devotion to frontier facts. Adams also showed a surprising range of humor, only hinted at in *The Log of a Cowboy*, with his 1906 collection of stories, *Cat-*

[6] *Ibid.*, 191.

tle Brands. In the collection, he also displays an unsuspected sympathy for the frontier woman, which leads to the belief that he could have written really well about the feminine side of the frontier if he had set himself to the task. But his best book remained *The Log of a Cowboy,* and if the cowboy is accepted as a major folk hero of the American people, then Adams' chronicle deserves to stand as a cornerstone of that heroic erection.

Unquestionably the best writer of the turn-of-the-century group was Eugene Manlove Rhodes, who for the past several years has been undergoing rediscovery—or in many instances, discovery. He knew the West—felt the West—as probably no other writing contemporary. Born in Nebraska, reared in Kansas, a horse wrangler at sixteen, a guide and scout in the Geronimo uprisings at seventeen, a cowboy and ranchman for twenty-five years, he wrote about a life he had lived and observed and heard about firsthand. Lacking a formal education, he compensated for this deficiency by wide and careful reading. He began to write for the *Saturday Evening Post,* at first in collaboration with Henry Wallace Phillips, who taught Rhodes whatever you can teach a natural artist about his craft. From the first decade of the twentieth century till Rhodes' death, the *Saturday Evening Post* was Rhodes' best outlet for publication and his best source of income, which was never sufficient.

Critics are divided on just how good Rhodes was. They agree he was a rare craftsman, but they also think he had more craft than heart. Bernard DeVoto makes this comment:

That is the generalization about Gene Rhodes: that his books are the only embodiment on the level of art of one segment of American experience. They are the only body of fiction devoted to the cattle kingdom which is both true to it and written by an artist in prose. Surely that is a great deal: to have given fiction its sole mature expression of one era in our past, one portion of the experience that has gone to make up America.[7]

Dobie argues both sides. He acknowledges that Rhodes possessed a genius for creating character through conversation, adding:

Aside from their inherent decency, their most distinguishing characteristic is the vivacity of their talk. It is never glib; it is often witty; it is uniformly natural. The culmination of the art of writing as Eugene Manlove Rhodes practices, so it seems to me, is in this talk.[8]

But on the other hand, says Dobie, "Rhodes was ample-natured, but he cannot be classed as great because his grasp was too often disproportionately short of the long reach. His fiction becomes increasingly dated."[9]

Rhodes also fell short in neglecting to consider the impelling power which the color and romance of the myths and legends of the cowboy hold over the imagination of the American follk. The realism of *Moby Dick* may contribute to that novel's value, but its mysticism and symbolism have made it great. And it is here that Rhodes fell down, that, in fact, the whole realm of cowboy fiction falls down, for the fiction of frontier days won't be truly accepted as classic unless and until the archetypal myths are woven into the story, for they are a part of the American folk mind.

Henry Wallace Phillips, Rhodes' sometime collaborator, achieved a measure of popularity that has proved ev-

[7] Mary Davison Rhodes, *The Hired Man on Horseback,* xxxix.
[8] Dearing (ed.), *The Best Novels,* xiii.
[9] Dobie, *Guide to Life and Literature of the Southwest,* 115.

anescent as the century grows older. Born in New York in 1869, the third year of the trail drives to Abilene, he worked several years in Canada and the Dakotas as a cowboy, miner, and schoolteacher. In 1902, he introduced the public to a cowboy hero named Red Saunders by way of a novel of the same name. Red was quickly accepted, as Phillips could write convincingly and create vital characters. Phillips deserves mention because he was one of the early writers to make *one* cowboy his fictional hero, and though his collection of stories might not be designated as art, his approach was in that direction.

One of the most prolific writers was Stewart Edward White, who included the cowboy in a whole motley host of subjects and came out with one story, "The Rawhide," which is a classic of sorts. White, a graduate of the University of Michigan with a year at Columbia Law School, lived four of his teen-age years on a California ranch and later prospected for gold in the Black Hills and hunted and camped periodically in California, Arizona, and Wyoming. Beginning in the first decade of the twentieth century, *McClure's Magazine* was the outlet for White's cowboy stories. In 1907, he brought out a collection, *Arizona Nights*, which shows his ability, like Wister's, to work with myths and legends which are accepted if not understood by the American folk.

"The Rawhide" is a story of Buck Johnson and his wife Estrella, whom he picked up through a Kansas City newspaper matrimonial advertisement. The vastness and isolation of the West depressed Estrella, who spent much of her time staring out into the view of nothing, of which the West has such quantity. She became fascinated by green rawhide and its contracting powers; she would tie strips around green gourds and choke them; and the tender barks of young cottonwoods were indented from her tying rawhide strips around their trunks. Estrella finally fell in love and departed with a young cowboy. Johnson pursued them, bound them together with green rawhide, and left them to die after the fashion of Estrella's little game back on the ranch. In the end, Buck Johnson relents and releases the pair, which weakens the story. In the meanwhile, however, White has told one of the really original stories of the Old West.

William Sidney Porter, who is not unknown as O. Henry, wrote forty stories against the Texas background in which he lived for fifteen years. He had come to Texas from South Carolina in 1882, when the West still possessed its frontier and when the broad-brimmed sombrero on the streets of Austin was no affectation. He learned to ride, to shoot from the saddle, and to break a bronco. Nineteen of his forty Texas stories appeared in *Heart of the West*, while others were interspersed through *Options*, *Roads of Destiny*, *Sixes and Sevens*, *Whirligigs*, and *Rolling Stones*. The West doesn't burn within the soul of the man whose name is usually mentioned with Poe's whenever American short story development is discussed, but he likes to tell of cowboys, Texas Rangers, ranchmen, sheepmen, and outlaws, and to use their locales for his settings.[10] And while O. Henry did not give the cowboy an enduring classic, he did write some charming stories and leave behind one outlaw character who apparently will endure, though the movies have changed him until O. Henry would hardly recognize him. This character, of course, is the Cisco Kid, whom O. Henry let roam free "because he could shoot five-sixths of a second sooner than any sheriff or ranger in the service, and because he rode a

[10] Robert H. Davis and Arthur B. Maurice, *The Caliph of Bagdad*, 18–19, 24. Fred Lewis Pattee, *The New American Literature, 1890–1930*, 167, 172.

speckled roan horse that knew every cowpath in the mesquite." [11]

Probably the most lasting O. Henry cowboy story was his "Hearts and Crosses," a typical O. Henry pudding contrived through a mixture of artful plotting, sympathy, and deft telling. It relates the story of a married man who comes to feel he is mainly a hired hand and very little of a man. He leaves his wife, a famous cattle queen, to become foreman at another ranch, from where he sends back an order for a number of cattle. One of the new purchases arriving from his wife is pure white except for an unusual brand—a cross in the center of a heart. Puzzled, he returns to find he is the father of a son. Whatever the story's charm, it illustrates as well as any O. Henry story that the great storyteller was more interested in using cattle and ranching for settings than in contributing anything to our knowledge of actual ranch life. Like so much of O. Henry, the story with slight shifts could as easily have taken place among miners or taxi drivers or millworkers as among cattle folk. The best O. Henry story of ranch life—perhaps the best short story wrapped around a ranch theme by any author anywhere—is his "Last of the Troubadours," but here O. Henry's ranch is a sheep, not a cattle, ranch.

Another writer worth mentioning among the better writers of the Western story is George Pattullo, the Canadian-born Bostonian who followed Erwin Smith to the West, recording mentally as the Texas artist recorded photographically. As Pattullo saw, he wrote, and he soon became one of George Horace Lorimer's prize producers of Western short stories for the *Saturday Evening Post*, which, incidentally, deserves more than a nod for popularizing the West with its wide circulation of Western fic-

[11] O. Henry, "The Caballero's Way," *The Complete Works of O. Henry*, 198.

tion. Under Lorimer's direction, the *Post* influenced writers to treat the cowboy with reasonable accuracy, to take the Western out of the strictly blood-and-thunder category, to wean the American magazine-reading public off the East Lynne and St. Elmo type of "mellowdrammer" and away from the comic antics of the Negro minstrels and so on, and to portray American life as it almost was lived.

Pattullo wrote for more than just the *Post*, however, and from 1908 on, his stories appeared all over the literary place. Enormously enthusiastic and almost equally enormously energetic, he was particularly good at writing of animals, especially of horses. Many of his stories followed along humorous lines, such as his story about Ol' Sam, the chuck wagon mule, whose appetite for bread led to his feud with the cook. A collection of Pattullo's stories from the *Post*, *McClure's*, and *American Magazine* were gathered into a book called *The Untamed*, which is about as rousing a collection as is likely to be found. Pattullo also turned out a novel, *The Sheriff of Badger Hole*, which showed that while Pattullo hadn't forgotten his West, he was capable of commercializing his product to suit the Eastern market.

One other superior writer in the period just after the turn of the century is Hamlin Garland, who grew up in Wisconsin and Iowa, where he tasted enough blowing dirt to write of the West with considerable fidelity and disenchantment from his sanctuary in the East. Although Garland is not usually thought of as a cowboy fiction writer, he gets into this study because of one book which appeared in 1916, *They of the High Trail*, which shows Garland at his most sober as well as, at times, his most melodramatic peak. Only *The Log of a Cowboy* was written with a similar feeling of artistic responsibility, for Garland had neither the humor of, say, Alfred Henry Lewis nor the popular appeal of a writer like Wister.

Garland is concerned with the range rider after the frontier era has moved on, at the same time recognizing that though frontier conditions may have passed, what has been left is still bound up with space and sparseness of human population and is not too far removed from the West that was. His two best stories in *They of the High Trail* are "The Remittance Man" and "The Trail Tramp."

"The Remittance Man" concerns a young Englishman of good family who comes West to learn the business of cattle raising. What he meets makes him recoil. Blondell, the rancher, has "the bearings of a dangerous old bear. His voice was a rumble, his teeth were broken fangs, and his hands resembled the paws of a gorilla." Mrs. Blondell was "big, fat, worried and complaining." Neither of them recognized dirt as anything but a friend. And daughter Fran was a lovely animal, but an animal, "not merely unkept, but smudgy." [12] In a reversal of the Molly Wood–Virginian story, the superior male begins to surrender to the uncultured Fran, with none of *The Virginian's* romanticism; and in the end, Fran reaches up to the Englishman, and he reaches down to the tasty, inviting animal. We can't say that we blame him, though the fear persists that twenty years hence she might be as big and fat and complaining as her mother.

Garland struck pay dirt of a sort with "Trail Tramp," which depicts Sulphur Springs in 1896 trying to get rid of the "wild West business" which insists in hanging on, helped along by the herders who "strove to keep up cowboy traditions by unloading [their Winchesters and revolvers] on the slightest provocation." Ed Kelley is hired as town marshal to bring order, and he brings it by meet-

[12] Hamlin Garland, *They of the High Trail*, 58.

ing one challenging cowboy after another, including "Clayt Mink . . . the worst little moth-eaten scrap in the state" who will "kill at the drop of a hat" and is determined to "try out this new marshal same as he did the others."[13] Kelley successfully defends himself against all antagonists, including Mink, after which he resigns for lack of support from the town board (the recently-issued movie, *High Noon,* a production of rare poetic spirit, worked closely to this same general plot). Garland panders in spots, but on the whole the story is quite conscientiously and artfully told.

So far in this chapter, we have pulled out several good-to-better authors—Wister, Adams, O. Henry, Garland among them. Nowadays, though, who reads them, outside of possibly O. Henry, who may be read for his all-around adroitness rather than for any Western predilections? The truth is, the better Western writers as a rule have the smaller audience, while others of less stature have become virtually household words and have continued to hold audiences. Millions of readers have been devoted to Zane Grey for more than fifty years. Mulford's Hopalong Cassidy novels and William MacLeod Raine's stories have remained on the reading lists almost as persistently as Grey's. It is they that the general public thinks of when it thinks of cowboy stories—and not a craftsman in the whole corral.

For any discussion of popular Western writers, Zane Grey is the necessary starting place. After more than a half century, his novels are still being reissued and are in constant demand in public and lending libraries. In the spring of 1955, a New York publishing house took full-page, back-cover color ads in a national periodical to advertise Grey's collected works in "One Magnificent

[13] *Ibid.,* 113.

Matched Library"—twenty-five volumes by Zane Grey, "Most beloved Western story teller of all times. The blood of Indian chiefs flowed through his veins, and he actually lived the rugged life made famous in his exciting books." It's none of our concern, but we'll wager that the publisher makes a pile of money bigger than a prickly pear thicket or buffalo chips at a prospective campfire.

Grey has been translated into Russian, French, and Spanish—and read. It might be obtuse to argue that his novels have literary merit, but it is likewise difficult to argue with such phenomenal success, for it puts the critic in the same position as the New York music critic who devastated, he thought, a certain toothsome, matinee-idol type who plays the piano and smiles to huge paying audiences, only to receive from that worthy a note saying how much the review had hurt his feelings—"I cried all the way to the bank!" There is little need to deprecate, or depreciate, Zane Grey's fiction. It's here and it's likely to remain, and the critic would be absurd who would deny that Grey lacks a certain significance. But what is that significance? Briefly, the significance is romance, which is another word for *escape.*

Grey's name itself suggests a certain romantic aura. Further, his titles are suggestive of a faraway West of old frontier days. Such titles as *Riders of the Purple Sage, The Lone Star Ranger, The Light of Western Stars, The Thundering Herd,* and *The Heritage of the Desert* seem to promise a story to lift you out of yourself for a few hours. Grey made some pretense at being historically accurate and failed, and that failure may be another explanation of his writing fortune, for facts never stood in the way of his exciting tales.

What this New York dentist-turned-writer did better than any other popular author of Western and cowboy fiction was to embrace in prose the common misconceptions which American folk consciousness had assigned to the Old West and give them color and action. His characters think but little, but they act much. Their emotions and passions, though noble at times, are definitely and invariably primitive. They represent the West where men are supposed to be men, and they fall, without perplexing intermediate shadings, into the categories of "good" or "bad." T. K. Whipple, who has written the only thoughtful analysis of Grey's novels, sees the author and his works in this light:

There is no reason for comparing him with anyone, unless perhaps with competitors in his own genre. If he must be classified, however, let it be with the authors of *Beowulf* and of the Icelandic sagas. Mr. Grey's work is a primitive epic, and has the characteristics of other primitive epics. His art is archaic, with the traits of all archaic art. His style, for example, has the stiffness which comes from imperfect mastery of the medium. It lacks fluency and facility; behind it always we feel a pressure toward expression, a striving for a freer and easier utterance. Herein lies much of the charm of all early art—in that technique lags somewhat behind the impulse.[14]

Grey may not have written literature of quality, but he wrote of just about every type of Westerner—cowboys, miners, Texas Rangers, and rustlers. For example, you might first experience Grey writing about a railroad in *The U. P. Trail.* The prospect of a story of a cattle-sheep feud leaves you cold, but you like Grey, and so you try his *To the Last Man.* You follow him down the Indian trail in *The Vanishing American.* Before long you will read about any aspect of Western life, so long as it is seen through the eyes of Grey. He may be no Henry James,

[14] *Study Out the Land,* 21.

Bret Harte, or Stephen Crane, but in the short run, at least, his impact on the American folk mind has been greater than that of those three, or of any other contemporary trio of authors combined. When you think of the West, you think of Zane Grey.

A man of considerably more modest output but who hit a popular chord in the first decade of the twentieth century was Frank Hamilton Spears, whose *Whispering Smith,* a best seller of 1908, has gone through at least three recognizable filmings by Hollywood and several reprintings to the present time. Spears, New York born, Wisconsin-educated, became a bank president who learned something about railroads through his financial relationships with them, and he wrote his best known fiction around railroad themes. *Whispering Smith* itself is a railroad story primarily, with the eponymous hero a former cowboy, who draws on his cowboy lore, especially his skill with a gun, to succeed as a railroad detective.

Of considerably more importance audience-wise is Clarence E. Mulford, whose Hopalong Cassidy stories have written one of the pages in American folk history. Mulford wrote his first cowboy stories before he had ever been West, but later occidental junkets in search of material failed to improve the reality of his stories. Nonetheless, his Cassidy and Bar 20 tales, first published in book form in 1907 and seen before that in *Outing Magazine,* have been made into at least twenty-five movies and have entranced no telling how many millions of readers. Their level is about the level of today's pulp fiction, with emphasis on violence, and from a literary or historical standpoint have nothing to recommend them. But the broad reading public doesn't pick up its taste from critics and academicians—nor, as we have seen, do the juveniles.

One of the best in the popular cowboy fiction field is a

woman, Mrs. Bertha Muzzy Sinclair, who also began her work in this century's first decade. Mrs. Sinclair, who wrote as B. M. Bower, had what so many cowboy writers lack, a real background of life among the bowlegged brethren. Born in Minnesota, she was reared in Montana, where she rode the range and fraternized with the men on horseback. From *Chip of the Flying U*, her first, down through a number of sequels, she wrote in a playful, humorous vein. She did not try to pontificate about the epic role of the cowboy, and she had no pretenses to history as such, but she was faithful to the Western historical milieu which she knew firsthand. J. Frank Dobie said he thought her novels almost as good as those of Eugene Manlove Rhodes, an opinion to which we would enter an exception.

Several other writers gave Western fiction a whirl with rather good commercial success and with some craftsmanship. Dane Coolidge brought out *Hidden Water*, an account of conflict between cattlemen and sheepmen, in 1910; the next year his *Texican* appeared. They were as good as anything else appearing in their day. William MacLeod Raine, English-born but Western-grown, wrote so well about the cowboy country he knew that the British soldiers in the trenches in World War I ordered 500,000 copies of his novels. He was less a writer than, say, Coolidge, but he was wise enough to work with the conventional materials which are a part of the cowboy lore. Rex Beach, who is associated with other violent fictional worlds, brought out in 1915 *Heart of the Sunset*. Zane Grey never did anything better, which is not as damning as it might seem.

Still other names could be mentioned: Charles Alden Seltzer, who wrote his novels in the strictly "wild and wooly" vein; Cyrus Townsend Brady, author of *Arizona* and *Westwind;* Herbert Myrick, who wrote the amusing melodrama, *Cache la Poudre: The Romance of a Tenderfoot in the Days of Custer;* and Roger Pocock, whose *Curly: A Tale of the Arizona Desert* grafts two feuding English families in a curious melodrama that labors to spill every last possible drop of blood from its participants.

The Englishmen picked up some market. Harold Bindloss of Liverpool wrote the *Cattle Baron's Daughter* about the cattle kings of the northern ranges and their resistance to the invading grangers. It reads as if Bindloss never left Liverpool. Ridgewell Cullum was a sort of English Zane Grey. One of his novels, *The Nightriders,* a conscious melodrama, is pretty good, if you like melodrama.

Along with the development of the cowboy novel came the cowboy juvenile. Beadle and Adams aimed a number of its novels at boys only, though there was no objection to adults' reading them. In this century, Andy Adams wrote *Wells Brothers, the Young Cattle Kings,* about the Wells brothers who were awarded trail cattle for providing a kind of refuge for trail drivers no longer able to continue with their trail herds. George Bird Grinnell wrote two excellent, highly factual novels for boys, *Jack, the Young Ranchman,* and *Jack, the Young Cowboy,* both of which have become standards. Grinnell set his stories in the Colorado ranch country and worked in game hunting adventures in the Colorado Rockies, a subject about which he knew a good deal. Joseph Bushnell Ames, a rather conventional juvenile writer, also had something of a vogue in the early 1900's, especially with his *Pete, Cowpuncher.*

The foregoing writers do not compose a definitive list of all the novelists and short story writers who treated the cattlemen's frontier in prose before 1915. A perusal of *The Saturday Evening Post* turns up such names, among others, as Eleanor Gates, William R. Lighton, and Al J.

Jennings, and the other periodicals pioneering in Western fiction can add other names almost *ad infinitum.* But the list here is reliable as far as it represents the major writers working in the cowboy genre. These writers did not necessarily write the best Western fiction, but they wrote the most influential, and a study of the hundreds of Western novels since 1915 would reveal little change in the pattern these men set.

These are the men who paved the way for such generally faithful novels as Hough's *North of 36* and Dorothy Scarborough's *The Wind* in the 1920's, and for such later fragile prose-poetry as Conrad Richter's *Sea of Grass,* Tom Lea's *The Wonderful Country,* Walter Van Tilburg Clark's *The Oxbow Incident* and *Track of the Cat,* John Steinbeck's *The Red Pony,* Jack Schaefer's *Shane,* and perhaps best of all, John Houghton Allen's *Southwest,* books with an almost filigree delicacy, books that can evoke mood pangs of almost ineffable anguish, books so exquisitely put together that they anger or hurt us more pedestrian writers—and yet books, too, that are descendants of the books of these same thirty or so early writers who realized that they had a heroic age in their awkward, often maudlin grasp and who set out with varying crudity to transfer some of that realization to the broader American public. Before dismissing the literary qualities of these writers, be it Webber, Wister, or Grey, let the critic remember that these were the men who opened up the West to literature. In a way, they, too, were pioneers.

11. The Critics

As both authors and readers are well aware, there exists no paucity of books and articles on the cowboy and the cattleman's frontier, written by everyone from the untrained, reminiscent, and too often inept local historian to the trained, and nearly as often inept, scholar. Likewise, a very large body of short stories and novels have traced the story of the cowboy on his open range. But little attention has been paid the critics of Western literature, those critics who have turned out a body of investigation running the gamut from good to poor. The look that follows does not pretend to be exhaustive, but it does lay a claim for uniqueness, in that almost no previous attempt has been made to bring together the best that has been thought and written about Western literature.

The starting place is naturally enough with J. Frank

Dobie, who vies with J. Evetts Haley as the man who looks most like a writer on Western subjects ought to. The word *dean* implies a certain dignity and even pomposity, both of which are about as far from Pancho Dobie's sham-shooting make up as Dallas is from Fort Worth culturally; but Dobie, nonetheless, wears the legitimate brand of dean of cowboy bibliographers and critics—the dean and the most respected, if not the most solemn, which is something else again. Until a cowboy work has received the Dobie accolade, it has not achieved its real knighthood, no matter how much it may be lauded on the front page of the New York *Times Book Review* or in the *Saturday Review*. And the impetus which he has given to the study of Southwestern culture has made him a figure of international standing. He is no Western apologist, and he is no Western chauvinist either.

Dobie's *Guide to Life and Literature of the Southwest* inspires that favorite bromide of reviewers—it is a "mine of information" about the literature of the Southwest, classified all sorts of ways and replete with literally hundreds of pungent Dobian comments on Western writers. Listen to these two as samples:

On *We Pointed Them North:*

Helena Huntington Smith, who actually wrote and arranged Teddy Blue's reminiscences, instead of currying him down and putting a checkrein on him, spurred him in the flanks and told him to swaller his head. He did.[1]

And on Frank Harris's *My Reminiscences as a Cowboy:*

A blatant farrago of lies, included in this list because of its supreme worthlessness.[2]

[1] Dobie, *Life and Literature of the Southwest,* 60.
[2] *Ibid.,* 64.

Dobie's comments on cowboy writers can be found all over the place. He is a soft touch for anyone who needs an introduction written, he is a frequent reviewer, and through the years he has written steadily for *Southwest Review* and for publications of the Texas Folklore Society, of which he has been the moving spirit and sometimes editor. When, during World War II, Cambridge University was looking for someone who could explain Britain's chief ally, it picked, not a historian or a political scientist, but J. Frank Dobie, a professor of English who had spent his life singing of cowboys, longhorns, coyotes, and mustangs, and of the men who write about them.

Whereas Dobie has strewn his opinions in books and periodicals all over the face of the nation, our second critic is known almost entirely for opinions expressed in one book. The critic is Douglas Branch, whose *The Cowboy and His Interpreters*, which appeared in 1926, has been a standard reference for nearly three decades. Branch is not without his faults, especially historically, as when he swallows the apocryphal story of the freighters who were forced to abandon their bull teams on the High Plains at the beginning of winter and returned in the spring to find them fat and healthy, thereby opening the northern ranges to exploitation by cattlemen.[3] He makes such errors of minutiae as to state that the "greatest of the dime-novel cowboys is Young Wild West,"[4] when as a matter of record Young Wild West did not begin to appear until three years after the dime novel had passed from the scene.[5]

Branch almost dismisses *The Virginian* as no cowboy story at all, since "there is not one scene set on the range among the cattle."[6] Dobie put it more vividly: the hero, he

[3] Douglas Branch, *The Cowboy and His Interpreters*, 107.
[4] *Ibid.*, 185.
[5] Henry Nash Smith, *Virgin Land*, 220.
[6] Branch, *The Cowboy*, 198.

says, "is a cowboy without cows . . . [who] does not even smell of cows." But Dobie then goes on to acknowledge that *The Virginian* "authentically realizes the code of the range, and . . . makes . . . absorbing reading," whereas Branch would like to rule it out of the cowboy club.[7] On the other hand, Branch stands on solid ground when he passes judgment on such books as Hough's *North of 36*, Rhodes' *West Is West*, and Adams' *Log of a Cowboy*, which he, like others, terms the best piece of literature which the cattle country has produced.

Most of the Western literary criticism tends toward the descriptive rather than the analytical. Walter Prescott Webb tried to combine the two approaches in his comprehensive chapter on Western literature in *The Great Plains*. Like Dobie, Webb is no man to apologize, and he is being his usual, straightforward self when he asserts that "an examination of the literature of the Great Plains indicates that there is in it a promise of something distinctive and American, as yet scarcely discerned";[8] and that it "would require an artist of the most consummate skill and genius to write a novel of the cattle country, however true to life it might be, that would not fall immediately under the curse of being 'another Western.' "[9] Webb, a historian by profession, is part poet and part mystic by nature, and he sees the West and its cattle kingdom through a gossamer curtain that softens and obscures the harshness which he knows from firsthand experience lies beyond that veil. After six decades of studying the West—he claims in all seriousness to have begun preparing for his life's work when he was four years old—he can still be thrilled by its story; and a really lyric chapter, such as Paul Horgan did

[7] Dobie, *Life and Literature of the Southwest*, 70–71.
[8] Webb, *The Great Plains*, 455.
[9] *Ibid.*, 462.

on the cowboy in his recent *Great River,* can send Webb soaring for days, in print and out.[10]

In 1938, Mabel Major, Rebecca Smith, and T. M. Pearce brought out *The Southwest Heritage,* a literary history and bibliography of the Southwest in which they included a chapter on the fiction of the cattle kingdom. Mostly, they merely mentioned the more notable works and reproduced certain criticisms by Dobie and Webb. However, they did point out that the "most original stories that the Southwest has told have come from the cattle country," while at the same time they doubted that much of artistic value had shown.[11]

A more thoughtful criticism is the one which W. H. Hutchinson published in *The Western Humanities Review* in 1949. Some of his criticism is simply attractive paraphrasing of Dobie, Webb, and Bernard DeVoto, but some of his other judgments are rather original. He calls *Wolfville* a "classic example of two-dimensional grotesquerie in western fiction . . . between Harte and Haycox," and credits George Pattullo not only with "fine writing and good reading," but with producing stories that "ring clear and true as shod hoof on malpais."[12]

Marshall Fishwick, who wrote a rather good examination of Billy the Kid in *The Saturday Review,* comparing the legend of that unworthy with the Faust legend, did not come out so well in another 1952 article, in which he tried to make a case for the cowboy as America's contribution to the world's mythology. Aside from calling attention to the cowboy's existence as a kind of myth, not only in American folklore, but in a far larger, international sense,

[10] Horgan, *Great River,* II, 871–86.
[11] Mabel Major, Rebecca Smith, and T. M. Pearce (eds.), *Southwest Heritage,* 80.
[12] W. H. Hutchinson, "The 'Western Story' as Literature," *Western Humanities Review,* Vol. III, No. 1 (January, 1949), 36.

he contributed little that wasn't already available in other places.[13]

No more interesting literary criticism of the cattle kingdom can be found than the two articles which Bernard DeVoto, a Utah-cum-Harvard writer of Western fiction, as well as a critic of wide interests and an expert on almost everything from kitchen knives upward, wrote for *The Saturday Review* some twenty years ago. DeVoto, who may be captious or cute but hardly dull, makes several statements designed to challenge his readers' thinking processes. Pointing out that "A boy old enough to drive a chuck wagon with the first herd of longhorns entrained at Abilene could have seen the rise and fall of the kingdom and still have been no more than middle-aged when it lapsed into legend," he goes on to say that the "cattle trade is the only American business which has evoked a literature, a mythology, and graphic symbolism of its own." At the "humblest level of this literature," says DeVoto, stands the cowboy story.[14] It is Devoto's opinion that if any significant literature of the Old West is ever written—and he himself has tried with some success, as in *Across the Wide Missouri*—the cattle kingdom will not supply the theme.[15] In fact, Eugene Manlove Rhodes, in DeVoto's opinion, has written the only cowboy fiction "that reaches a level which it is intelligible to call art." [16] Incidentally, DeVoto's observations on the literature of the cattle kingdom in his introduction to *The Hired Man on Horseback* comprise as trenchant an appraisal as can be found.

The myth of the cowboy gets attention from Mody

[13] Fishwick, "The Cowboy: America's Contribution to the World's Mythology," *Western Folklore*, Vol. XI, No. 2 (April, 1952), 77–92.

[14] "Horizon Land (1)," *Saturday Review of Literature*, Vol. XIV, No. 25 (October 17, 1936), 8.

[15] DeVoto, "Horizon Land (2)," *Saturday Review of Literature*, Vol. XV, No. 26 (April 24, 1937), 8.

[16] Rhodes, *The Hired Man on Horseback*, xxxi.

Boatright, a member of the same University of Texas Department of English in which Dobie once rapped for attention. Boatright recognizes the cowboy as a popular folk hero who possesses two qualities which all folk heroes have in common: prowess and cleverness. Boatright also takes Wister apart with some distinction. Wister's cowboys, he says, are natural gentlemen, but Wister at the same time accepts the postulate of Herbert Spencer, William Graham Sumner, and Charles Darwin that there is going to be a "best" man who will win in society's ceaseless struggle for survival. Wister, says Boatright, supported the theory of Anglo-Saxon superiority and the racial inferiority of Negroes and Indians, and was obviously anti-Semitic. While Boatright accepts the cowboy as a folk hero, he doesn't find it "altogether reassuring that in a time of greater complexity and greater insecurity than Wister lived to see, the cowboy with his six-shooter, his simple ethics, and his facility for direct action is our leading folk hero." [17] As part of an article he wrote on literature in the Southwest, Boatright also criticized the cowboy, but he added little that was new.[18]

One of the more provocative books of the past several years is *Virgin Land* by Henry Nash Smith, who passed through such universities as Southern Methodist, Texas, and Minnesota en route to California (as of this moment). Smith also joins the throng in designating the cowboy as "the dominant type" in American folklore.[19] Despite his designation, however, Smith devotes less than three pages to the cowboy, though he does take time to make one contribution by tracing the myth concept of the frontier West

[17] Boatright, "The American Myth Rides the Range," *Southwest Review*, Vol. XXXVI, No. 3 (Summer, 1951), 163.
[18] Boatright, "Literature in the Southwest," Sul Ross State College *Bulletin*, Vol. XXXIII, No. 2 (June, 1953), 12.
[19] Smith, *Virgin Land*, 109.

through Daniel Boone, Leatherstocking, Kit Carson, Deadwood Dick, Buffalo Bill, and Buck Taylor.

The literary criticisms which have appeared about Zane Grey have ranged from near libel to guarded appraisals. Branch quotes these lines in his account of the critics' attitudes toward Grey:

> A man whom few there are to love,
> And none who dare to shoot.[20]

Typical of this school of thought is Burton Rascoe, who made the following comment about the popularity and merit of Zane Grey's novels:

Of these writers, Zane Grey who had an estimated fifty-four million readers for his fifty-four published books (he left completed manuscripts of two novels) was a star. It is difficult to imagine any writer having less merit in either style or substance than Grey and still maintain an audience at all. . . .[21]

On the other hand, T. K. Whipple has raised a strong voice in support of Grey, as in the following statement:

Mr. Grey has received justice only from his millions of devoted readers—and some of them, I fear, have been shamefaced in their enthusiasm. The critics and reviewers have been persistently upstage in their treatment of Mr. Grey; they have lectured him for lacking qualities which there was no reason for him to possess, and have ignored most of the qualities in which he is conspicuous.[22]

Whipple, we suspect, was trying to formulate an opinion. Rascoe was satisfied with a prejudice.

[20] *The Cowboy*, 250.
[21] "Opie Read and Zane Grey," *Saturday Review of Literature*, Vol. XXI, No. 3 (November 11, 1939), 8.
[22] *Study Out the Land*, 19–20.

The critics aren't numerous. The few that do exist tend to fall into one of three categories: those who neither laud nor condemn, but just describe, going out on a critical limb no farther than to praise *The Log of a Cowboy*, which is every bit as daring as defending God and Home; those who approach the Western genre with dignity and a sense of responsibility—Webb and Whipple belong in this class; and those who dismiss the Western story out of a personal literary pique that tells them that nothing west of Pittsburgh or south of Jersey can have any validity unless it reeks of starving sharecroppers, senseless segregation, or sadistic sex.

Yet the fact remains that, critic or no, the American cowboy retains his place at the head of this nation's folk heroes, and that criticism of cowboy literature has barely begun to emerge from a state comparable with that occupied by the cowboy fiction practitioners at the turn of the century. The critics agree that the cowboy has significance and vitality. They don't agree on what that significance is, and they don't agree either on how the cowboy's writers handle him. But they are beginning to take the cowboy seriously, and a better critical age may lie just ahead.

12. The Truthtellers

As we have progressed along our pedestrian way in this narrative of mounted men, we have tried to keep a reasonably objective middle ground on the subject of the cowboy, realizing that nothing so promotes academic pedestrianism as that sainted shibboleth of "objectivity," but realizing also that too many writers on cowboy subjects either fall "head over heels" in love with their broad-brimmed heroes or else visit the other extreme of all but outlawing the cowboy as unfit for human society. But in our attempt to walk the fence between the myth and the reality of the cowman, we are not alone, nor first on the scene by any means.

Through the years, there have been a number of men who could look at the cowboy, not exactly with disenchantment, but with clarity and comprehension nonetheless. There have been men who have seen the cowboy in larger relationships—as a descendant perhaps of the medieval knight on horseback (the man of action, of course; astride a horse, of course; wearing a striking occupational garment unlike that of the earthbound legions about him, of course; and, of course, adept with a special weapon), or as a contemporary of his Australian cousin, who also ranged over vast areas trailing cattle under conditions not dissimilar to those in the West—and not one whit easier, or as another contemporary to his even more romantic *pariente*, the gaucho from the Argentine pampas, who could teach his North American *primo* something about the handling of nomadic cattle, the riding of hell-bent horses, and beyond that, the loneliness of space and the bigness of loneliness. And especially there have been writers who saw the cowboy in a narrower, strictly American sense, but who within their limits were faithful reporters.

Several writers, such as Dobie and Webb, have already been treated in considerable detail. But there are others, publishing particularly with the university presses of the Southwest, who have apparently dedicated their writing lives to damming the stream of unreality inundating the Old West and then carefully examining the fields of cowboy truth. They take the cowboy seriously, but not so seriously as to magnify him beyond reasonable proportion. They seem to feel that if they keep the steady light of truth trained on the film of cowboy life, occasionally a print will emerge from the confused negative that will show the picture as it really should be—clear and lifelike and with some dimension and heart.

Passing by Dobie (about whom you really couldn't say too much), the most notable of the truthtellers is undoubtedly J. Evetts Haley. Although this stringbean West Texan likes to stalk publicly such unmounted game as university professors and social democracies, controversial targets at best and worse than controversial when Haley gets through with them, there is no controversy when Haley completes his account of a ranch, a rancher, or a peace officer, or of a slice of Western history. He simply wraps up that subject for the ages. In prose that is as economical as he wants his government to be and that some how manages to be simultaneously as sharp-etched as his drought-ridden ranchland and as colorful as one of his summer sunsets, Haley goes after his subject of the moment with the pace and with the authority that comes from living with what he is talking about.

In *The XIT Ranch of Texas*, first published in 1929, Haley not only told the truth but told the whole truth so wholly that the book had to be withdrawn from circulation under threat of libel. It reappeared more than two decades later, but by then the passage of time and the omission of certain spade callings made its contents non-litigious. His *Charles Goodnight, Cowman and Plainsman,* a biography of real proportions about one of the major figures in Western ranching, could almost serve as a textbook on ranching, its paragraphs bristling with the sort of unobtrusive details that come only from absolute familiarity with an environment. It is noteworthy, but not at all surprising, that Haley's *Goodnight* and his later *George W. Littlefield, Texan,* books marketed strictly for their depiction of colorful, important ranchmen, are such complete expositions of ranch life that they comprise two of the four ranch listings of a recent comprehensive bibliography devoted solely to books on American business.[1]

[1] Henrietta M. Larson, *Guide to Business History*, 114–15. A third Haley book, Charles Schreiner, *General Merchandise: the Story of a*

Curiously, Haley is quite likely to be most remembered for a book of pictures, for he wrote the text for the incomparable Erwin Smith photographs comprising *Life on the Texas Range*, a book which Dobie called "easily the finest range book in the realm of the pictorial ever published" and a book which shows the true cowboy—a man on horseback, but a man working.[2] In every word, whether he is utilizing his spare prose to amplify one of Smith's pictures of cowboys tallying for the trail, or is writing more vividly of that "world of dry air and shimmering light that shriveled the skins but freed the souls of venturesome men who loved and lived with horses," or is distinguishing "the light-riding, genuine cowhand from the soggy-seated country boy draped like a bag of mush all over his horse and saddle," Haley's knowledgeable devotion to the cowboy is effectively apparent.[3] Combined, Haley and Dobie cover the Texas cowboy completely, Haley from his background of "undulating seas of grass" and Dobie from out of his Nueces brush origins. Both men see the whole cowboy, not the caricature shown on the screen or between book covers, and they see him with sympathy and with admiration, but without sentimentality. In Texas or beyond, Haley and Dobie represent the best contemporary work being done in the cowboy field.

Country Store, which is not without its dependence on cattle, is also included in Miss Larson's *Guide* (p. 98). No better indication of Haley's closeness to the range appears than in his opening sentences in *Charles Goodnight*: "This book," writes Haley, "is more than the biography of a man—it is the background of my own soil, a part of my own tradition. Every wind that drifts the alkali dust from the Goodnight Trail across my home range suggests a land of cattle and horses; every damp breeze carries the penetrating fragrance of greasewood, suggestive of the bold life that rode along it." (P. ix.)

[2] Dobie, *Guide to Life and Literature of the Southwest*, 119.

[3] Erwin E. Smith and J. Evetts Haley, *Life on the Texas Range*, 17, 20.

Not by any means, however, does this unyokeable pair possess a monopoly on the proper portrayal of the Old West and its cowboy hero. Between themselves, for instance, Wayne Gard and Sam P. Ridings have wrapped up the Chisholm Trail for at least a generation. Without embroidery of any kind, they have told the tale of the foremost cattle trail. Their two books are accurate in detail and, more important, accurate in the larger picture of the cowboy at his work.

Other more or less definitive books on various phases of the cowboy's life have appeared. In 1929, Ernest Staples Osgood, in his *Day of the Cattleman,* told the complete story of the development, with emphasis on economics, of the northern ranges. In 1954, the book was reissued with not a word changed nor fact amplified—since, really, little change was necessary. Osgood told his truths dispassionately—and in his instance, the truth has stood up for a quarter of a century.

Angie Debo has edited *The Cowman's Southwest,* Ora Brooks Peake has fenced off *The Colorado Range Cattle Industry,* and Louis Pelzer has analyzed the economics of *The Cattlemen's Frontier* thoroughly. All of these works are full and constant—and unimaginative, like so many of the western books published by the Arthur H. Clark Company. Except for possibly Miss Debo's book (in which, it must be said, she is at the mercy of her cowboy), the books are dependable, but like so many dependable things, including human beings, rather devoid of interest. Theirs represents a case in point for complaint—too many of the truthtellers get so immersed in fact that they fail to sell their briefs to the reading jury, which turns in boredom to the prostituted, but infinitely more interesting, commercial mythmakers. Edward Everett Dale, who also possesses a penchant for cowboy eco-

nomics, packages his written product much more inter-
estingly.

California, whose ranching lore has considerable antiquity, as American cattle ranging goes, but which, for a
state with its spread-eagle propensities, has curiously
failed to market this aspect of its frontier development, has
produced two writers on cowboy subjects who help to lead
the reader down the true trail. Robert Glass Cleland,
whose intellectual range is as vast as the West which
fascinates him, contributed an unarguable picture of pre-
Civil War ranching in his *The Cattle on a Thousand Hills*.
And Jo Mora, who is not the scholar that Cleland is, but
whose comprehension of the California cowboy exceeds
his colleague's, has put together two fine books in *California*, which treats incidentally of the West Coast
vaquero, and *Trail Dust and Saddle Leather*, which is primarily concerned with the cowman and his gear.

Back in Texas, Ramon Adams is gradually encom-
passing the cowboy, one facet at a time, with enthusiasti-
cally careful books covering a range from trail cookery to
cowboy lingo to Western gunmen, horsed and unhorsed.
At the opposite end of the state from the Dallas business-
man-author works C. L. Sonnichsen, whose primary interest is folklore but who brings facility to anything he
essays, as in his far-ranging *Cowboys and Cattle Kings*,
which, through its portrayal of the contemporary cattleman, reveals much lore concerning the cowboy of the past.
Sonnichsen might be criticized for exploring too widely to
get down any real roots to his story, but he is to be extended a definite credit for having brought off an attempt
to show the cowboy as he is, instead of as he is exhibited
at the box office and book stall.

In San Antonio, Chris Emmett has told the story of
Shanghai Pierce: A Fair Likeness. Pierce, a South Texas

cowman who could be ruthless, expansively good-humored, audacious, and invariably successful, all at the same time, almost upsets the theme of this book, for he was a fictional type incarnate, and Emmett's unsparing account reads like fiction. The accounts of how Pierce bilked a Kansas cow trader named Black and of how he kept books on Charlie Siringo deserve a place in the permanent folklore of the range.[4]

Near the true geographical center of Texas, which Texans appropriately call West Texas, with central Texas at least a hundred miles to the eastward, works Fred Gipson, whose reputation lies mainly in the fictional field but who extends verity whenever he writes about cattle, whether it be his straightforward accounts of Fat Alvord in *Cowhand* and Zack Miller in *Fabulous Empire,* or the show-off bronc buster, Ruel MacLaurin, in *Recollection Creek,* and old Sam Goodall, the camp cook, in his delightful children's book (which will probably prove even more delightful to adults), *The Trail-driving Rooster.*

For the whole truth, one Texas magazine is absolutely essential, and another may attain essentiality. The necessary magazine is *The Cattleman,* published in Fort Worth and now, in 1955, in its forty-second year. *The Cattleman* is primarily what its title implies, a periodical for cattlemen, and is as filled with articles of interest only to practicing cowmen, as *Editor and Publisher* is with articles for journalists only, or *Today's Woman* with recipes and homemaking. But scattered throughout its issues, *The Cattleman* carries reminiscences and memoirs and articles of historical interest that, in the aggregate, give an unimpeachable picture of the practicing cowhand of other decades.

---

[4] Chris Emmett, *Shanghai Pierce: A Fair Likeness,* 54–56. Siringo also tells this story in the several editions of his autobiography.

Down in Austin, which is neither cowtown nor western, Joe Small is in his second year of publishing *True West* as a bimonthly. Although Small goes far beyond the cattle range in his search for western materials, he brings in the cowboy and the range in his search for the true West in which the cowboy played such a major role. Apparently Small has hit a responsive reading chord, for his magazine has grown steadily in circulation despite his steadfast opposition to slick commercialization. When in January, 1955, Small suggested that he might "jazz up" his magazine a bit for a wider readership, the response was a small deluge. One reader in Oklahoma said: "Stick to the Old West. Tell the truth about it. There's so many yarns printed, so many lies, so much hog-wash about the Old West . . . the true stories of the Old West are long overdue." Letters from the two coasts and from the Gulf to Canada, as well as from Germany and Sweden, echoed this same sentiment, though usually with more restraint. So for the nonce, *True West* continues as a source of cowboy lore as the cowboy lived it—and not as some Hollywood cowboy lived it up!

And speaking of sources, historians place great store by primary sources—by accounts as told or written by persons who lived through an era. The reminiscing cowboy explodes any inherent value of such primary sources, for nobody can wander farther from the truth than the aging cowboy—or even the not-too-aged one—who has sat around successive superheated cowboys' reunions at Stamford and swapped and amplified yarns until he can no longer distinguish between the events he participated in in New Mexico and some narratives that found their way down from Montana. Thus the dozens of variations on the life of Billy the Kid, who is about to be resurrected again, and thus the less colorful and equally unnecessary confusion of John Chisum and Jesse Chisholm, who operated worlds apart in distance and in magnitude.[5]

But because some memoirs are so totally confused, and therefore inadmissible as historical or mythological evidence, does not mean that all memoirs are to be discarded. All should be suspect, but so should the memoirs of chairmen of important Senate committees or of name-dropping society dowagers. But once the reader develops some ability to distinguish between the authentically colorful and the colorfully windy, he can learn substantially about life on the open range as seen through the eyes and the memories of the men who lived that life.

Operating at a somewhat elevated level in the field of memoirs are such former cowmen as John Culley, the Oxford-educated New Mexico rancher, whose *Cattle, Horses, and Men* reveals a man of intellectual breadth to match his experiences; John Clay, a highly successful manager of several large British-owned Western ranches, whose *My Life on the Range* gives as complete and as proper a picture of ranch life as can be found; Frank S. Hastings, who knew his cattle from both the meat packing and the meat producing sides, and who told his story with mellow vividness in *A Ranchman's Recollections* (for facets of ranch life in the Big Pasture country that no one else has touched, read especially Hastings' short chapters on "The Storm," "Old Gran'pa," and "The Speckled Yearlin'," chapters without pose or defense, and every bit as honest as Hastings' orphan cowboy when he admitted to the quiet grandstand that he "jest had to ride" that steer: "I needed them boots and thet John B., so's I could be a real cowboy, an' this yere speckled yearlin's done done it."); Granville Stuart, whose *Forty Years on the Frontier* is the notable

[5] C. L. Sonnichsen, *Alias Billy the Kid*. (Albuquerque, University of New Mexico Press, 1955).

exception to the charge made a few pages back that Arthur H. Clark's publications defer toward dullness; or Peter Wright, still another Britisher, who, in his *A Three-Foot Stool*, displayed a catholicity of understanding that is virtually unmatched in cowboy literature. These men had amplitude, urbanity, and intellectual sophistication, in the better sense of that overworked and overrated word.

Below these works in grace and perspective, but with the same devotion to imaginative truth, are such rousing recollections as that disarmingly frank one, sex-wise, told by E. C. "Teddy Blue" Abbott, *We Pointed Them North.* Abbott, who became Granville Stuart's son-in-law, once he settled down, has given a narration that is just plain fun to read. The only memoir to equal it for sheer delight is the first of the cowboy autobiographies, Charles A. Siringo's *A Texas Cowboy*, whose subtitle, *Fifteen Years on the Hurricane Deck of a Spanish Cow Pony,* gives an idea of the author's impertinent and robust attitude toward his vocation. If for no other reason Siringo should be remembered as an author who wrote one of the very few truly honest prefaces. "My excuse," he began, "for writing this book is money—and lots of it." Reading the *Police Gazette* had awakened his hunger for the things that money could buy—and that he couldn't—since, to use his own words, "the days of honorable cattle stealing is past." In 1885, he turned his "mind into a healthier channel" and produced a book that became known as the cowboys' Bible, which went through any number of reprintings and new editions, which, according to Dobie, had the "virtue [of being] written and published without benefit of respectability," and which deserves just about everything nice which has been said about it (though *nice* is a somewhat precious word to use in connection with anything describing the rowdy Siringo).

Just as genuine but not quite so highly seasoned are any number of other memoirs. To name four, there is James Emmit McCauley's *A Stove-Up Cowboy's Story*, which deserves to be described by another overworked word—it is inimitable, the sort of book that you may open abstractedly anywhere along the way and wind up reading both forward and back till you've finished it at one sitting. Patrick T. Tucker's *Riding the High Country* not only gives an intimate picture of the author's life as a cowman but also gives further insight into that greatest of rangeland painters, Charles M. Russell, whose stature continues to grow yearly, except among certain artistic cults who look on anything painted last year as hopelessly outdated. Bruce Sibert's notes on his life on the Dakota range, which have been put together by Walker D. Wyman in *Nothing but Prairie and Sky*, display an unfailing good humor as well as a close acquaintance with cow and horse culture. And finally, James H. Cook's *Fifty Years on the Old Frontier* is a deserved standard on cowboy work in the brush country in the 1870's.

To close this brief roundup of the truthtellers, no more appropriate book could here be branded than Joseph G. McCoy's *Historic Sketches of the Cattle Trade of the West and Southwest*, the first of the whole cow lot. McCoy, as much responsible as any one man can be for the shape and scope the trailing of range cattle took, wrote his story from the vantage points of a man who had been singularly associated with the bringing of Texas cattle northward, who had been conditioned by success turned to failure—conditioned but never disillusioned nor really disappointed, and who turned an ever fresh and inquiring eye on this phenomenon he had helped to create. Although McCoy is not always correct in his details, and many of his errors of fact have been perpetuated by hasty historians, from the larger view of the cowboy at work and the cowboy at play, McCoy has absolute honesty and dependability. One rather recent (1940) edition of McCoy's *Sketches*, by far outstripping all the others, including the original, which first appeared more than eighty years ago, is the Arthur H. Clark edition which Ralph Bieber has edited and enlarged with his wisdom derived from years spent among Western materials. The combination of McCoy and Bieber results in a story of prime quality and significance.

Here, then, are a few of the men who have written about the cowboy, either in fiction or in fact, in truth or in distortion. From almost any direction you wish to approach the cowboy, they cover the range. Some of them are avowedly sentimental, others unwittingly so; some are disenchanted, some downright antipathetic; and some are frankly commercial, while others are at least striving to present a portrait and not a caricature.

On the sentimental side, but nonetheless fittingly tender, is the tribute which Charles Goodnight paid his colleagues of another day:

I wish I could find words to express the trueness, the bravery, the hardihood, the sense of honor, the loyalty to their trust and to each other of the old trail hands [wrote Goodnight]. They kept their places around a herd under all circumstances, and if they had to fight they were always ready. Timid men were not among them—the life did not fit them. I wish I could convey in language the feeling of companionship we had for one another. Despite all that has been said of him, the old-time cowboy is the most misunderstood man on earth. May the flowers prosper on his grave and ever bloom, for I can only salute him—in silence.[6]

[6] Haley, *Charles Goodnight*, 466.

His modern counterpart may be a better educated and a better (here goes another awful word) integrated workman who can do more with greater facility; the modern steer may weigh twice what the old longhorn did, horns included (though we'll wager the longhorn tasted better, what with so many modern cattle being fattened beyond good savor); and the fence may have brought order and economy to cow breeding and raising; but the old-time brush popper will never meet his superior, in modern days, for ability to take hard, lonely work, day in and day out, in heat sizzle or in the teeth of a norther moving in like a blue darter. Twelve hours in the saddle, two hours' watch at night, plus interruptions which might consume most of the remainder of the night, night after night; the same unimaginative chuck to eat and the same hard ground to sleep on for weeks, or even months, on end; low pay and nothing to spend it for except the occasional binge in some raw town—this was the cowboy's life. About the only comparable life within recent memory would be that of some rusting sailor stuck away on a destroyer in a desolate sector of MacArthur's Southwest Pacific, where there was nothing to do except work, where work seemed eternal, and where prolonged sleep was something you thought about but seldom experienced.

But despite the hardships, despite the inconvenience, and despite the danger, few cowboys would have chosen any other life. Few indeed would have agreed with one of their fellows, Jim McCauley, when he wrote the following, after he had become a "stove-up" cowboy:

All in all I got out of cowpunching is the experience. I paid a good price for that. I wouldn't take anything for what I have saw but I wouldn't care to travel the same road again, and my advice to any young man or boy is to stay at home and not be a rambler, as it won't buy you anything. And above everything stay away from a cow ranch, as not many cowpunchers ever save any money and 'tis a dangerous life to live.

. . . when it rains I don't have to hurry to get my slicker on and get to my night horse to go hold a herd of wild, stampeded cattle, but just sleep on. And I don't have to ride horses that it takes three or four men to hold while I put the saddle on and while I crawl up in the saddle. All in all, I'll just as soon to farm.[7]

Even McCauley contradicted himself and more nearly expressed the old-time cowboy's viewpoint when later he wrote to John A. Lomax as follows:

I wish I had never saw a cow ranch. . . . While Ide rather be on a cow ranch and work just wages, . . . than anything you could name . . . the wild free life whare you have to feel if your closest friend is still on your hip, . . . and if your old horse will make it in, and to make the Mexico line and get back without any holes in your hide—that is real living, that is sport, but 'tis the violant kind and lots of people love it beyond a doubt.[8]

Yes, most waddies would tell you, that *was* real living, that *was* sport, and they loved it—"beyond a doubt!"

And so, clad in his boots and chaps, armed with his six-shooter, and stone broke, the Western cowboy rides gloriously on, riding not into the limbo of the past but apparently, more vigorous than ever, into the long future. The range rider is a myth, but he is a myth possessing a living and present reality in the American folk mind. Condemn him, deprecate him, dismiss him, distort him, even

[7] *A Stove-Up Cowboy's Story,* 72–73.
[8] *Ibid.,* xvii.

set the dogged historian to work on him—and for all the disapproval which may be marshaled and for all the dead hands of fact which may be laid over his body, nothing shall avail to cancel half a line of what the American public is pleased to believe about him.

Bibliography

Primary Sources

Periodicals

Bell, James G. "A Log of the Texas-California Cattle Trail," edited by J. Evetts Haley, *Southwestern Historical Quarterly*, Vol. XXXV, No. 3 (January, 1932), 208–37.

The Cattleman. 41 vols. Fort Worth, Texas, 1915–1954.

Cook, James H. "The Texas Trail," *Nebraska History Magazine*, Vol. XVI, No. 4 (October–December, 1937), 229–40.

Cronin, Con P. "Arizona's Six Gun Classic," *Arizona Historical Review*, Vol. III, No. 2 (July, 1930), 7–11.

Duffield, George C. "Driving Cattle from Texas to Iowa, 1866," edited by W. W. Baldwin, *Annals of Iowa*, Vol. XIV, No. 4 (April, 1924), 243–62.

McGOUGH, W. C. "Driving Cattle into Old Mexico in 1864," *West Texas Historical Association Year Book*, Vol. XIII. (October, 1937), 112–121.

ROOSEVELT, THEODORE. "Ranch Life in the Far West," *The Century Magazine*, Vol. XXXV, No. 4 (February, 1888), 495–510.

———. "Sheriff's Work on a Ranch," *The Century Magazine*, Vol. XXXVI, No. 1 (May–October, 1888), 40–51.

SAUNDERS, GEORGE W. "Old Time Trail Drivers of Texas," *West Texas Historical Association Year Book*, Vol. V (June, 1929), 130–31.

"Two City Marshals," *Transactions of the Kansas Historical Society*, Vol. IX (1905–1906), 526–40.

WILKESON, FRANK. "Cattle Raising on the Plains," *Harper's Monthly Magazine*, Vol. LXXII (April, 1886), 285–90.

Books

ABBOTT, E. C. ("Teddy Blue"), and HELENA HUNTINGTON SMITH. *We Pointed Them North*. New York, Farrar & Rinehart, Inc., 1939.

ABERNATHY, JOHN R. *In Camp with Theodore Roosevelt*. Oklahoma City, Oklahoma, The Times-Journal Publishing Co., 1933.

ALDRIDGE, REGINALD. *Ranch Notes*. London, Longmans, Green and Co., 1884.

ANDERSON, J. W. *From the Plains to the Pulpit*. [Addicks, Texas, Myrtle Anderson], 1907.

BARNARD, EVAN G. *A Rider of the Cherokee Strip*. Boston, Houghton Mifflin Company, 1936.

BARNES, WILL C. *Apaches and Longhorns*. Los Angeles, The Ward Ritchie Press, 1941.

BENTON, JESSE JAMES. *Cow by the Tail*. Boston, Houghton Mifflin Company, 1943.

BEVERLY, BOB. *Hobo of the Rangeland*. Lovington, New Mexico, Leader Publishing Company, [1940].

BRATT, JOHN. *Trails of Yesterday*. Chicago, University Publishing Company, 1921.

BUNTON, MARY TAYLOR. *A Bride on the Old Chisholm Trail in 1886*. San Antonio, Texas, The Naylor Company, 1939.

CLAY, JOHN. *My Life on the Range*. Chicago, privately printed, 1924.

COE, GEORGE W. *Frontier Fighter*. Albuquerque, University of New Mexico Press, 1951.

COOK, JAMES H. *Fifty Years on the Old Frontier*. New Haven, Yale University Press, 1923.

COWAN, BUD. *Range Rider*. Garden City, N. Y., Doubleday, Doran & Company, Inc., 1930.

CULLEY, JOHN H. *Cattle, Horses & Men of the Western Range*. Los Angeles, California, The Ward Ritchie Press, 1940.

CUTBIRTH, RUBY NICHOLS. *Ed Nichols Rode a Horse*. Dallas, University Press, 1943.

DEBO, ANGIE (ed.). *The Cowman's Southwest, Being the Reminiscences of Oliver Nelson*. Glendale, California, The Arthur H. Clark Company, 1953.

DONOHO, M. H. *Circle-Dot*. Topeka, Crane & Company, 1907.

GARRETT, PAT F. *The Authentic Life of Billy the Kid*. Norman, University of Oklahoma Press, 1954.

GILLETT, JAMES B. *Six Years with the Texas Rangers*. Austin, Von Boeckmann-Jones Co., 1921.

GREEN, RENA MAVERICK (ed.). *Samuel Maverick, Texan: 1803–1870*. San Antonio, 1952.

GUERNSEY, CHARLES A. *Wyoming Cowboy Days*. New York, G. P. Putnam's Sons, 1936.

HALSELL, H. H. *Cowboys and Cattleland*. Nashville, Tenn., The Parthenon Press, n.d.

HINKLE, JAMES FIELDING. *Early Days of a Cowboy on the Pecos*. Roswell, New Mexico, 1937.

HOYT, HENRY F. *A Frontier Doctor*. Boston, Houghton Mifflin Company, 1929.

HUNTER, JOHN MARVIN. *The Trail Drivers of Texas*. Nashville, Cokesbury Press, 1925.

JAMES, W. S. *Cow-Boy Life in Texas*. Chicago, M. A. Donohue & Co., 1893.

Kansas Pacific Railway Company. *Guide Map of the Best and*

Shortest Cattle Trail to the Kansas Pacific Railway. [Fort Worth, Texas], Kansas Pacific Railway Co., 1875.

KING, FRANK MARION. *Longhorn Trail Drivers.* Los Angeles, Haynes Corporation, 1940.

———. *Wranglin' the Past.* Pasadena, California, Trail's End Publishing Co., Inc., 1946.

KUPPER, WINIFRED (ed.). *Texas Sheepman: The Reminiscences of Robert Maudslay.* Austin, University of Texas Press, 1951.

LANG, LINCOLN A. *Ranching with Roosevelt.* Philadelphia, J. B. Lippincott Company, 1926.

LEWIS, WILLIE NEWBURY. *Between Sun and Sod.* Clarendon, Texas, Clarendon Press, 1938.

MANDET-GRANEY, E. de, *Cow-boys and Colonels.* New York, E. P. Dutton & Company, n.d.

McCAULEY, J. E. *A Stove-Up Cowboy's Story.* Austin, Texas, Texas Folklore Society, 1943.

McCOY, JOSEPH G. *Historic Sketches of the Cattle Trade of the West and Southwest.* Edited by Ralph P. Bieber. Glendale, California, The Arthur H. Clark Company, 1940.

McINTIRE, JIM. *Early Days in Texas; A Trip to Hell and Heaven.* Kansas City, Mo., McIntire Publishing Company, 1902.

MERCER, A. S. *The Banditti of the Plains.* San Francisco, The Grabhorn Press, 1935.

MOORE, JOHN M. *The West.* (Wichita Falls, Texas), Wichita Printing Company, 1935.

O'KEEFE, RUFUS W. *Cowboy Life.* San Antonio, Texas, The Naylor Company, 1936.

OTERO, MIGUEL ANTONIO. *My Life on the Frontier 1864–1882.* New York, The Press of the Pioneers, 1935.

———. *My Life on the Frontier 1882–1897.* Albuquerque, The University of New Mexico Press, 1939.

———. *The Real Billy the Kid.* New York, Rufus Rockwell, Inc. 1936.

PONTING, TOM CANDY. *Life of Tom Candy Ponting: An Autobiography.* Evanston, Illinois, The Branding Iron Press, 1952.

Post, C. C. *Ten Years a Cowboy*. Chicago, Rhodes & McClure Publishing Company, 1901.

Potter, Jack Myers. *Cattle Trails of the Old West*. Clayton, New Mexico, Laura R. Krehbiel, 1939.

Price, Con. *Trails I Rode*. Pasadena, California, Trail's End Publishing Co., Inc., 1947.

Rhodes, Mary Davison. *The Hired Man on Horseback: My Story of Eugene Manlove Rhodes*. Boston, Houghton Mifflin Company, 1938.

Ricketts, William Pendleton. *50 Years in the Saddle*. Sheridan, Wyoming, Star Publishing Company, 1942.

Rollinson, John K. *Wyoming Cattle Trails*. Caldwell, Idaho, The Caxton Printers, Ltd., 1948.

Roosevelt, Theodore. *An Autobiography*. New York, Charles Scribner's Sons, 1929.

———. *Ranch Life and the Hunting Trail*. Philadelphia, Gebbie and Company, 1903.

Rush, Oscar. *The Open Range*. Caldwell, Idaho. The Caxton Printers, Ltd., 1936.

Sage, Lee. *The Last Rustler: The Autobiography of Lee Sage*. Boston, Little, Brown and Company, 1930.

Siringo, Charles A. *A Texas Cowboy*. New York, William Sloane Associates, Inc., 1950.

Smith, Erwin Evans, and J. Evetts Haley. *Life on the Texas Range*. Austin, University of Texas Press, 1952.

Stuart, Granville. *Forty Years on the Frontier*. 2 vols. Cleveland, The Arthur H. Clark Company, 1925.

Thorp, N. Howard. *Pardner of the Wind*. Caldwell, Idaho, The Caxton Printers, Ltd., 1945.

Thwaites, Reuben G. (ed.). *Early Western Travels, 1748–1846*. 32 vols. Cleveland, The Arthur H. Clark Company, 1904–1907.

Tucker, Patrick T. *Riding the High Country*. Caldwell, Idaho, The Caxton Printers, Ltd., 1933.

Wright, Peter. *A Three-Foot Stool*. New York, E. P. Dutton & Company, 1909.

Wright, Robert M. *Dodge City, the Cowboy Capital*. Wichita, Kansas, Wichita Eagle Press, 1913.

Secondary Materials

"The American Cowboy Still Dominates His Own and Other Industries," *Newsweek,* Vol. XXXVII (June 18, 1951), 56–59.

ASHTON, JOHN. "The Texas Cattle Trade in 1870," *The Cattleman,* Vol. XXXVIII, No. 2 (July, 1951), 21, 74–75.

BAUMANN, JOHN. "On a Western Ranche," *Fortnightly Review,* Vol. XLVII (1887), 516–33.

BLACKMAR, FRANK W. "The History of the Desert," *Transactions of the Kansas State Historical Society,* Vol. IX (1905–1906), 101–14.

BOATRIGHT, MODY C. "The American Myth Rides the Range," *Southwest Review,* Vol. XXXVI, No. 3 (Summer, 1951), 157–63.

————. "Literature in the Southwest," *Sul Ross State College Bulletin,* Vol. XXXIII, No. 2 (June 1, 1953), 1–32.

————. "The Myth of Frontier Individualism," *Southwestern Social Science Quarterly,* Vol. XXII (June, 1941), 14–32.

BOTKIN, J. T. "Conquering a Day When Cowboys Were Cowboys," *Kansas Historical Collections,* Vol. XVI (1923–1925), 493–96.

BRIGGS, HAROLD E. "Early Freight and Stage Lines in Dakota," *North Dakota Historical Quarterly,* Vol. III (October, 1928–July, 1929), 229–61.

CUSHMAN, GEORGE L. "Abilene, First of the Kansas Cowtowns," *Kansas Historical Quarterly,* Vol. IX, No. 3 (August, 1940), 240–58.

DALE, EDWARD EVERETT. "The Cow Country in Transition," *Mississippi Valley Historical Review,* Vol. XXIV (June, 1937–March, 1938), 3–20.

————. "The Romance of the Range," *West Texas Historical Association Year Book,* Vol. V (June, 1929) 3–22.

DEVOTO, BERNARD. "Horizon Land (1)," *Saturday Review of Literature,* Vol. XIV, No. 25 (October 17, 1936), 8.

————. "Horizon Land (2)," *Saturday Review of Literature,* Vol. XV, No. 26 (April 24, 1937), 8.

DICK, EVERETT. "The Long Drive," *Kansas Historical Collections,* Vol. XVII, (1926–1928), 27–97.

DOBIE, J. FRANK. "Andy Adams, Cowboy Chronicler," *Southwest Review*, Vol. XI, No. 2 (January, 1926), 92–101.

———. "Billy the Kid," *Southwest Review*, Vol. XIV, No. 3 (Spring, 1929), 314–20.

———. "The First Cattle in Texas and the Southwest Progenitors of the Longhorns," *Southwestern Historical Quarterly*, Vol. XLII, No. 3 (January, 1939), 171–97.

———. "Tom Candy Ponting's Drive of Texas Cattle to Illinois," *The Cattleman*, Vol. XXXV, No. 8 (January, 1949), 34–45.

DORAN, THOMAS F. "Kansas Sixty Years Ago," *Kansas Historical Collections*, Vol. XV (1919–1922), 482–501.

FISHWICK, MARSHALL [W.]. "Billy the Kid: Faust in America," *Saturday Review*, Vol. XXV (October 11, 1952), 11–12, 34–36.

———. "The Cowboy: America's Contribution to the World's Mythology," *Western Folklore*, Vol. XI, No. 2 (April, 1952), 77–92.

FRENCH, WARREN. "The Cowboy in the Dime Novel," *Studies in English*, Vol. XXX (1951), 219–34.

GARD, WAYNE. "The Shawnee Trail," *Southwestern Historical Quarterly*, Vol. LVI, No. 3 (January, 1953), 359–77.

GRAHAM, PAULINE. "Novelist of the Unsung," *The Palimpsest*, Vol. XI, No. 2 (February, 1930), 67–77.

GROHMAN, W. BAILLIE. "Cattle Ranches in the Far West," *Fortnightly Review*, Vol. XXXIV (1880), 438–57.

HARGER, CHARLES MOREAU. "Cattle-Trails of the Prairies," *Scribner's Magazine*, Vol. XI (1892), 732–42.

HARVEY, CHARLES M. "The Dime Novel in American Life," *Atlantic Monthly*, Vol. C (July, 1907), 37–45.

HAVINS, T. F. "Sheepmen-Cattlemen Antagonisms on the Texas Frontier," *West Texas Historical Association Year Book*, Vol. XVIII (October, 1942), 10–23.

HAYTER, EARL W. "Barbed Wire Fencing—A Prairie Invention," *Agricultural History*, Vol. XIII, No. 4 (October, 1939), 189–207.

HOLT, R. D. "From Trail to Rail in Texas Cattle Industry," *The Cattleman*, Vol. XVIII, No. 10 (March, 1932), 50–59.

HOLT, R. D. "The Introduction of Barbed Wire Into Texas and the Fence Cutting War," *West Texas Historical Association Year Book*, Vol. VI (June, 1930), 65–79.

HUTCHINSON, W. H. "The 'Western Story' as Literature," *Western Humanities Review*, Vol. III, No. 1 (January, 1949), 33–37.

JACKSON, JOHN B. "Ich bin ein Cowboy aus Texas," *Southwest Review*, Vol. XXXVIII, No. 2 (Spring, 1953), 158–63.

KNAUTH, PERCY. "Gene Autry, Inc.," *Life*, Vol. XXIV (June 28, 1948), 89–100.

LOVE, CLARA M. "History of the Cattle Industry in the Southwest," *Southwestern Historical Quarterly*, Vol. XX, No. 1 (July, 1916), 1–18.

NIMMO, JOSEPH, JR. "The American Cowboy," *Harper's New Monthly Magazine*, Vol. LXXIII (November, 1886), 880–84.

OWSLEY, FRANK L. "The Pattern of Migration and Settlement on the Southern Frontier," *Journal of Southern History*, Vol. XI, No. 2 (May, 1945), 147–76.

RASCOE, BURTON. "Opie Read and Zane Grey," *Saturday Review of Literature*, Vol. XXI, No. 3 (November 11, 1939), 8.

RITCHIE, E .B. "A Trail Driver Who Kept a Diary," *The Cattleman*, Vol. XIX, No. 3 (August, 1932), 14–20.

RISTER, CARL COKE, "Outlaws and Vigilantes of the Southern Plains, 1865–1885," *Mississippi Valley Historical Review*, Vol. XIX (1932–1933), 537–54.

———. "The Significance of the Destruction of the Buffalo in the Southwest," *Southwestern Historical Quarterly*, Vol. XXXIII, No. 1 (July, 1929), 34–49.

SCHEIN, HARRY (Ida M. Alcock, transl.). "The Olympian Cowboy," *The American Scholar*, Vol. XXIV, No. 3 (Summer, 1955), 309–20.

SHARNIK, JOHN. "It's Go Western for Young Men," *New York Times Magazine*, September 24, 1950, 16–22.

SMITH, REBECCA W. "The Southwest in Fiction," *Saturday Review of Literature*, Vol. XXV (May 16, 1942), 12–13, 37.

STREETER, FLOYD BENJAMIN. "Ellsworth as a Texas Cattle Market," *Kansas Historical Quarterly*, Vol. IV, No. 4 (November, 1935), 338–98.

———. "Famous Cattle Drives," *The Cattleman*, Vol. XXXIV, No. 8 (January, 1948), 130–33.

———. "The National Cattle Trail," *The Cattleman*, Vol. XXXVIII, No. 1 (June, 1951), 26–27, 59–74.

THOMAS, CHAUNCEY. "Frontier Firearms," *Colorado Magazine*, Vol. VII, No. 3 (May, 1930), 102–109.

TREXLER, H. A. "The Buffalo Range of the Northwest," *Mississippi Valley Historical Review*, Vol. VII, No. 4 (March, 1921), 348–62.

WALLACE, WILLIAM SWILLING. "Short-Line Staging in New Mexico," *New Mexico Historical Review*, Vol. XXVI, No. 2 (April, 1951), 89–100.

WEBB, WALTER PRESCOTT, "The American Revolver and the West," *Scribner's Magazine*, Vol. LXXXI (January–June, 1927), 171–78.

WYMAN, WALKER D. "Bullwhacking: A Prosaic Profession Peculiar to the Great Plains," *New Mexico Historical Review*, Vol. VII, No. 4 (October, 1932), 297–310.

YOST, GENEVIEVE. "History of Lynching in Kansas," *Kansas Historical Quarterly*, Vol. II, No. 2 (May, 1933), 182–219.

Books

ADAMS, RAMON F. (Comp.) *Six-Guns & Saddle Leather: A Bibliography of Books and Pamphlets on Western Outlaws and Gunmen*. Norman, University of Oklahoma Press, 1954.

———, and HOMER E. BRITZMAN. *Charles M. Russell, The Cowboy Artist*. Pasadena, California, Trail's End Publishing Co., Inc., 1948.

AGATHA, SISTER M. *Texas Prose Writings*. Dallas, Banks Upshaw and Company, 1936.

ALLEN, LEWIS F. *American Cattle: Their History, Breeding, and Management*. New York, D. D. T. Moore, 1871.

ARNOLD, OREN, and JOHN P. HALE. *Hot Irons: Heraldry of the Range*. New York, The Macmillan Company, 1940.

BANNING, WILLIAM, and GEORGE HUGH BANNING. *Six Horses*. New York, The Century Co., 1950.

BECHDOLT, FREDERICK R. *Tales of the Old Timers*. New York, The Century Co., 1924.

BILLINGTON, RAY ALLEN. *Westward Expansion.* New York, The Macmillan Company, 1949.

BORDECHE, MAURICE, and ROBERT BRASILLACH. *The History of the Motion Pictures.* New York, W. W. Norton and Company, 1938.

BRANCH, DOUGLAS, *The Cowboy and His Interpreters.* New York, D. Appleton and Company, 1926.

BRAYER, GARNET M., and HERBERT O. BRAYER. *American Cattle Trails, 1540–1900.* Bayside, New York, American Pioneer Trails Association, 1952.

BRIGGS, HAROLD. *Frontiers of the Northwest.* New York, D. Appleton-Century Company, 1940.

BRUCE, PHILLIP ALEXANDER. *Economic History of Virginia in the Seventeenth Century.* New York, Macmillan Company, 1896.

CARLSON, RAYMOND (ed.). *Gallery of Western Paintings.* New York, McGraw-Hill Book Company, Inc., 1951.

COLLINGS, ELLSWORTH, and ALMA MILLER ENGLAND. *The 101 Ranch.* Norman, University of Oklahoma Press, 1938.

COOLIDGE, DANE. *Arizona Cowboys.* New York, E. P. Dutton and Co., Inc., 1938.

———. *Old California Cowboys.* New York, E. P. Dutton and Co., Inc., 1939.

———. *Texas Cowboys.* New York, E. P. Dutton & Co., Inc., 1937.

COX, JAMES. *Historical and Biographical Record of the Cattle Industry and the Cattlemen of Texas.* St. Louis, Woodward and Tiernan Printing Co., 1895.

CLELAND, ROBERT GLASS. *The Cattle on a Thousand Hills.* San Marino, California, The Huntington Library, 1951.

CRAIGIE, WILLIAM A., *et al.* (eds.). *A Dictionary of American English.* 2 vols. Chicago, University of Chicago Press, 1940.

CROSS, JOE. *Cattle Clatter.* Kansas City, Mo., Walker Publications, Inc., 1938.

CUNNINGHAME GRAHAM, R. B. *The Horses of the Conquest.* Norman, University of Oklahoma Press, 1949.

DALE, EDWARD EVERETT (ed.). *Frontier Trails: Autobiography of Frank M. Canton.* Boston, Houghton Mifflin Company, 1930.

———. *The Indians of the Southwest.* Norman, University of Oklahoma Press, 1949.

———. *The Range Cattle Industry.* Norman, University of Oklahoma Press, 1930.

DARBY, WILLIAM. *The Immigrant's Guide.* New York, Kirk and Mercein, 1818.

DAVIS, ROBERT L., and ARTHUR B. MAURICE. *The Caliph of Bagdad.* New York, D. Appleton and Company, 1931.

DENHARDT, ROBERT MOORMAN. *The Horse of the Americas.* Norman, University of Oklahoma Press, 1947.

DICK, EVERETT. *The Sod House Frontier, 1854–1890.* New York, D. Appleton-Century, 1937.

———. *Vanguards of the Frontier.* New York, D. Appleton Century, 1941.

DOBIE, J. FRANK. *Guide to Life and Literature of the Southwest.* Dallas, Southern Methodist University Press, 1943.

———. *Guide to Life and Literature of the Southwest.* Dallas, Southern Methodist University Press, 1952.

———. *The Longhorns.* Boston, Little, Brown and Company, 1941.

———. *The Mustangs.* Boston, Little, Brown and Company, 1952.

———. *A Vaquero of the Brush Country.* Dallas, The Southwest Press, 1929.

DYKES, J. C. *Billy the Kid: The Autobiography of a Legend.* Albuquerque, University of New Mexico Press, 1952.

DOUGLAS, C. L. *Cattle Kings of Texas.* Dallas, Cecil Baugh, 1939.

EMMETT, CHRIS. *Shanghai Pierce: A Fair Likeness.* Norman, University of Oklahoma Press, 1953.

GARD, WAYNE. *The Chisholm Trail.* Norman, University of Oklahoma Press, 1954.

———. *Frontier Justice.* Norman, University of Oklahoma Press, 1949.

GIPSON, FRED. *Cowhand.* New York, Harper & Brothers, 1953.

HAFEN, LeROY R. *The Overland Mail, 1849–1869.* Cleveland, The Arthur H. Clark Company, 1926.

——, and CARL COKE RISTER. *Western America.* New York, Prentice-Hall, Inc., 1941.

HALEY, J. EVETTS. *Charles Goodnight, Cowman and Plainsman.* Boston, Houghton Mifflin Company, 1936. Norman, University of Oklahoma Press, 1949.

——. *The XIT Ranch of Texas.* Chicago, The Lakeside Press, 1929. Norman, University of Oklahoma Press, 1953.

HAMNER, LAURA V. *Short Grass and Longhorns.* Norman, University of Oklahoma Press, 1943.

HASTINGS, FRANK S. *A Ranchman's Recollections.* Chicago, Illinois, The Breeder's Gazette, 1921.

HEBBARD, GRACE RAYMOND, and E. A. BRININSTOOL. *The Bozeman Trail.* 2 vols. Cleveland, The Arthur H. Clark Company, 1922.

HENRY, STUART. *Conquering Our Great American Plains.* New York, E. P. Dutton and Co., Inc. 1930.

HORGAN, PAUL. *Great River: The Rio Grande in North American History.* 2 vols., New York, Rinehart & Company, Inc., 1954.

HOLDEN, WILLIAM CURRY. *Rollie Burns.* Dallas, Texas, The Southwest Press, 1932.

——. *Spur Ranch.* Boston, The Christopher Publishing House, 1934.

HOUGH, E[MERSON]. *The Story of the Cowboy.* New York, D. Appleton and Company, 1898.

——. *The Story of the Outlaw.* The Outing Publishing Company, 1907.

HUNT, FRAZIER. *Cap Mossman.* New York, Hastings House, 1951.

——. *The Long Trail from Texas.* New York, Doubleday, Doran and Company, Inc., 1940.

JOHANNSEN, ALBERT. *The House of Beadle and Adams and Its Dime and Nickel Novels.* 2 vols. Norman, University of Oklahoma Press, 1950.

KUNTZ, STANLEY J., and HOWARD HAYCROFT (eds.). *Twentieth Century Authors*. New York, The H. W. Wilson Company, 1942.

LAKE, STUART N. *Wyatt Earp: Frontier Marshal*. Boston, Houghton Mifflin Company, 1931.

LARSON, HENRIETTA M. *Guide to Business History*. Cambridge, Massachusetts, Harvard University Press, 1948.

LEACH, JOSEPH. *The Typical Texan: Biography of an American Myth*. Dallas, Southern Methodist University Press, 1952.

LEWIS, WILLIE NEWBURY. *Between Sun and Sod*. Clarendon, Texas, Clarendon Press, 1938.

McCRACKEN, HAROLD. *Portrait of the Old West*. New York, McGraw-Hill Book Company, Inc., 1952.

MAJOR, MABEL, REBECCA W. SMITH, and G. M. PEARCE (eds.). *Southwest Heritage*. Albuquerque, University of New Mexico Press, 1938.

MATTISON, FRANK TEMPERLEY. *A History of the Episcopal Church in Northwest Texas*. Austin, Texas (M.A. Thesis, University of Texas), 1955.

MERIWETHER, ROBERT L. *The Expansion of South Carolina, 1729–1765*. Kingsport, Tennessee, Southern Publishers, Inc., 1940.

MORA, JO. *California*. Garden City, New York, Doubleday & Company, Inc., 1949.

———. *Trail Dust and Saddle Leather*. New York, Charles Scribner's Sons, 1946.

NIMMO, JOSEPH, JR. *Range and Ranch Cattle Traffic*. Washington, D. C., *Executive Document No. 267*, House of Representatives, 48th Congress, 2nd Session, 1885.

NORDYKE, LEWIS. *Cattle Empire, The Fabulous Story of the 3,000,000 Acre XIT*. New York, W. Morrow, 1949.

OSGOOD, ERNEST STAPLES. *The Day of the Cattleman*. Minneapolis, University of Minnesota Press, 1929 and 1954.

PANNELL, WALTER. *Civil War on the Range*. Los Angeles, Calif., Welcome News, 1943.

PATTEE, FRED LEWIS. *The New American Literature*. New York, The Century Co., 1930.

PEAKE, ORA BROOKS. *The Colorado Range Cattle Industry.* Glendale, California, Arthur H. Clark Company, 1937.

PEARCE, WILLIAM M. *A History of the Matador Land and Cattle Company, Limited, From 1882 to 1915.* Austin, Texas (Ph.D. Thesis, University of Texas), 1952.

PELZER, LOUIS. *The Cattleman's Frontier.* Glendale, California, The Arthur H. Clark Company, 1936.

Prose and Poetry of the Livestock Industry of the United States. Denver, National Live Stock Historical Association, 1905.

RAINE, WILLIAM MACLEOD, and WILL C. BARNES. *Cattle, Cowboys and Rangers.* New York, Grosset & Dunlap, 1930.

RICHARDSON, RUPERT NORVAL. *The Comanche Barrier to South Plains Settlement.* Glendale, California, The Arthur H. Clark Company, 1933.

———. *Texas: The Lone Star State.* New York, Prentice-Hall, Inc., 1943.

RIDING, SAM R. *The Chisholm Trail.* Guthrie, Oklahoma, Co-Operative Publishing Company, 1936.

RISTER, CARL COKE. *The Southwestern Frontier,* Cleveland, The Arthur H. Clark Company, 1936.

ROE, FRANK GILBERT. *The Indian and the Horse.* Norman, University of Oklahoma Press, 1955.

ROGERS, JOHN WILLIAM. *Finding Literature on the Texas Plains.* Dallas, Texas, The Southwest Press, 1931.

ROLLINS, PHILIP ASHTON. *The Cowboy.* New York, Charles Scribner's Sons, 1930.

———. *Jinglebob.* New York, Charles Scribner's Sons, 1930.

SCHAFER, JOSEPH. *The Social History of American Agriculture.* New York, The Macmillan Company, 1936.

SMITH, HENRY NASH. *Virgin Land: The American West as Symbol and Myth.* Cambridge, Harvard University Press, 1950.

SONNICHSEN, A. L. *Alias Billy the Kid.* Albuquerque, University of New Mexico Press, 1955.

———. *Cowboys and Cattle Kings.* Norman, University of Oklahoma Press, 1950.

STREETER, FLOYD BENJAMIN. *Prairie Trails and Cow Towns.* Boston, Chapman and Grimes, 1936.

TOWNE, CHARLES WAYLAND, and EDWARD NORRIS WENTWORTH. *Shepherd's Empire.* Norman, University of Oklahoma Press, 1945.

TRUETT, VELMA STEVENS. *On the Hoof in Nevada.* Los Angeles, Lorrin L. Morrison, 1950.

TURNER, FREDERICK JACKSON. *The Frontier in American History,* New York, Henry Holt Company, 1920.

VAN DOREN, CARL. *Secret History of the American Revolution.* New York, The Viking Press, 1951.

VESTAL, STANLEY. *Queen of Cowtowns: Dodge City.* New York, Harper & Brothers, 1952.

————. *Short Grass Country.* New York, Duell, Sloan & Pearce, 1941.

WAGONER, JUNIOR JEAN. *History of the Cattle Industry in Southern Arizona, 1540–1950.* Tucson, University of Arizona, 1952.

WALLACE, ERNEST, and E. ADAMSON HOEBEL. *The Comanches: Lords of the South Plains.* Norman, University of Oklahoma Press, 1952.

WEBB, WALTER PRESCOTT. *The Great Plains.* Boston, Ginn and Company, 1931.

————. *The Texas Rangers.* Boston, Houghton Mifflin Company, 1935.

WELLMAN, PAUL I. *Glory, God and Gold: A Narrative History.* Garden City, N. Y., Doubleday and Company, 1954.

————. *The Trampling Herd.* New York, Carrick & Evans, Inc., 1939.

WHIPPLE, T. K. *Study Out the Land.* Berkeley, University of California Press, 1943.

WILCOX, R. TURNER. *The Mode in Footwear.* New York, Charles Scribner's Sons, 1948.

WILLARD, JAMES F., and COLIN B. GOODYKOONTZ (eds.). *The Trans-Mississippi West.* Boulder, University of Colorado, 1930.

WILLIAMS, J. W. *The Big Ranch Country*. Wichita Falls, Texas, Terry Brothers, Printers, 1954.

WILLIAMSON, HAROLD F. *Winchester, The Gun That Won the West*. Washington, D. C., Combat Forces Press, 1952.

WYLLYS, RUFUS K. *Arizona: The History of a Frontier State*. Phoenix, Hobson and Herr, 1950.

Fiction—Short Stories

FOOTE, MARY HALLOCH. "A Touch of Sun," *Century Magazine*, Vol. LIX, No. 3 (January, 1900), 339–50; Vol. LIX, No. 4 (February, 1900), 551–58.

"'The Kid': A Chapter of Wyoming," *Lippincott's Magazine*, Vol. XXVII (February, 1881), 276–84.

OSBOURNE, F. M. "Sargent's Rodeo," *Lippincott's Magazine*, Vol. XXV (January, 1880), 9–20.

"Over Sunday at New Sharon," *Scribner's Monthly*, Vol. XIX, No. 5 (March, 1880), 768–75.

WISTER, OWEN. "How Lin McLean Went East," *Harper's New Monthly Magazine*, Vol. LXXXVI, No. DXI (December, 1892), 135–46.

Fiction—Books

ADAMS, ANDY. *Cattle Brands: A Collection of Western Camp-Fire Stories*. Boston, Houghton Mifflin Company, 1906.

———. *The Log of a Cowboy*. Boston, Houghton Mifflin Company, 1903 and 1931.

———. *The Outlet*. Boston, Houghton Mifflin Company, 1905.

———. *Reed Anthony, Cowman: An Autobiography*. Boston, Houghton Mifflin Company, 1907.

———. *A Texas Matchmaker*. Boston, Houghton Mifflin Company, 1904.

———. *Wells Brothers, The Young Cattle Kings*. Boston, Houghton Mifflin Company, 1911.

ALLEN, JOHN HOUGHTON. *Southwest*. Philadelphia, J. B. Lippincott Company, 1952.

BEACH, REX. *Heart of the Sunset*. New York, Harper & Brothers, 1915.

BINDLOSS, HAROLD. *The Cattle Baron's Daughter*. New York, Grosset & Dunlap, 1906.

BOATRIGHT, MODY C. *Tall Tales from Texas*. Dallas, The Southwest Press, 1934.

BOWER, B. M. (BERTHA MUZZY SINCLAIR). *Chip of the Flying U*. New York, G. W. Dillingham Company, 1906.

BRADY, CYRUS TOWNSEND. *Arizona: A Romance of the Great Southwest*. New York, Dodd, Mead and Company, 1914.

———. *The Westwind*. Chicago, A. C. McClurg and Co., 1912.

BRONSON, EDGAR BEECHER. *Cowboy Life on the Western Plains*. New York, George H. Doran Company, 1910.

CHITTENDEN, WILLIAM LAWRENCE. *Ranch Verses*. New York, G. P. Putnam's Sons, 1893.

CLARK, WALTER VAN TILBURG. *The Ox-Bow Incident*. New York, Random House, 1940.

———. *The Track of the Cat*. New York, Random House, 1949.

COOLIDGE, DANE. *Hidden Water*. Chicago, A. C. McClurg and Co., 1910.

———. *The Texican*. Chicago, A. C. McClurg and Co., 1911.

CULLUM, RIDGEWILL. *The Nightriders*. Philadelphia, G. W. Jacobs and Co., 1913.

DEARING, FRANK V. (ed.). *The Best Novels and Stories of Eugene Manlove Rhodes*. Boston, Houghton Mifflin Company, 1949.

ELLIS, EDWARD S. *Cowman and Rustlers*. Philadelphia, Henry G. Coates and Co., 1894.

GANN, WALTER. *The Trail Boss*. Boston, Houghton Mifflin Company, 1937.

GARLAND, HAMLIN. *They of the High Trail*. New York, Grosset & Dunlap, 1914.

GIPSON, FRED. *Recollection Creek*. New York, Harper & Brothers, 1955.

———. *The Trail-Driving Rooster*. New York, Harper & Brothers, 1955.

GREY, ZANE. *The Light of Western Stars*. New York, Grosset & Dunlap, 1914.

GREY, ZANE. *The Lone Star Ranger.* New York, Harper & Brothers, 1915.

GRINNELL, GEORGE BIRD. *Jack, The Young Cowboy.* New York, Frederick A. Stokes Company, 1913.

———. *Jack, The Young Ranchman.* New York, F. A. Stokes Company, 1899.

HOUGH, EMERSON, *Heart's Desire.* New York, The Macmillan Company, 1905.

———. *The Girl at the Halfway House.* New York, D. Appleton and Company, 1900.

———. *North of 36.* New York. D. Appleton and Company, 1924.

LEA, TOM. *The Wonderful Country.* Boston, Little, Brown and Company, 1952.

LEWIS, ALFRED HENRY. *Faro Nell and Her Friends.* New York, G. W. Dillingham Company, 1913.

———. *Wolfville.* New York, F. A. Stokes Company, 1923.

———. *Wolfville Days.* New York, F. A. Stokes Company, 1902.

———. *Wolfville Folks.* New York, The Macaulay Company, 1908.

———. *Wolfville Nights.* New York, F. A. Stokes Company, 1902.

McELRATH, FRANCES. *The Rustler, A Tale of Love and War in Wyoming.* New York, Funk and Wagnalls Company, 1902.

MILLER, LEWIS B. *Saddles and Lariats.* Boston, Dana Estes and Company, 1912.

MORECAMP, ARTHUR. [Pseudonym for Thomas Pilgrim.] *Live Boys: Or Charley and Nasho in Texas.* Boston, Lee and Shepard, 1880.

———. *Live Boys in the Black Hills.* Boston, Lee and Shepard, 1880.

MYRICK, HERBERT. *Cache La Poudre: The Romance of a Tenderfoot in the Days of Custer.* New York, Orange Judd Company, 1905.

[O. HENRY.] *The Complete Works of O. Henry.* Garden City, New York, Garden City Publishing Co., Inc., 1937.

PATERSON, ARTHUR. *A Son of the Plains.* New York, Macmillan and Company, 1895.

PATTULLO, GEORGE. *The Sheriff of Badger Hole.* New York, D. Appleton and Company, 1912.

————. *The Untamed.* New York, Desmond City Herald, Inc., 1908.

PHILLIPS, HENRY WALLACE. *Red Saunders.* New York, McClure, Phillips and Co., 1902.

POCOCK, ROGER. *Curly: A Tale of the Arizona Desert.* Boston, Little, Brown and Company, 1905.

RHODES, EUGENE MANLOVE. *Good Men and True.* New York, Henry Holt and Company, 1910.

RICHTER, CONRAD. *The Sea of Grass.* New York, Alfred A. Knopf, 1937.

SCARBOROUGH, DOROTHY. *The Wind.* New York, Harper & Brothers, 1925.

SCHAEFER, JACK WARNER. *Shane.* Boston, Houghton Mifflin Company, 1954.

SEELY, HOWARD. *A Lone Star Bo-Peep and Other Tales of Texas Ranch Life.* New York, W. L. Mershon and Co., 1885.

————. *A Ranchman's Stories.* New York, Dodd, Mead & Company, 1886.

SPEARS, FRANK HAMILTON. *Whispering Smith.* New York, Charles Scribner's Sons, 1906.

STEINBECK, JOHN. *The Red Pony.* New York, The Viking Press, 1945.

TWAIN, MARK. *Roughing It.* New York, Grosset & Dunlap, 1913.

WEBBER, CHARLES W. *Tales of the Southern Border.* Philadelphia, Lippincott, Grambo & Co., 1853.

WHITE, STEWART EDWARD. *Arizona Nights.* New York, The McClure Company, 1908.

WINTHROP, THEODORE. *John Brent.* Boston, Ticknor and Fields, 1862.

WISTER, OWEN. *The Jimmyjohn Boss.* New York, Harper & Brothers, 1900.

WISTER, OWEN. *Lin McLean.* New York, Harper & Brothers, 1898.

———. *A Member of the Family.* New York, The Macmillan Company, 1911.

———. *The Virginian.* New York, Grosset & Dunlap, 1931.

Index

Cattlemen's associations: 57, 106ff.; in Texas, 106; in Wyoming, 106–107
Chicago, Illinois: 27, 31f., 71
Cibola: 20
Civil War: 15, 26
Clark, Richard (Deadwood Dick): 9, 125, 145
Clark, Walter Van Tilburg: 177
Clay, John: 35, 195
Cleland, Robert Glass: 192
Cody, William F. (Buffalo Bill): 70f., 121–23, 145–46
Coe, Phil: 90f.
Collins, Joel: 72
Colorado: 51
Colt revolver: 72, 77ff., 84ff.
Colt, Samuel: 84f.
Columbus, Christopher: 20, 23
Cook, James H.: 197
Cooke, Jay: 17
Coolidge, Dane: 175
Cooper, James Fenimore: 8
Coronado: 18, 20
Cowboys: activities of, 7; as folk hero, *ix*, 7, 8, 14, 33, 49, 81; dress of, 78ff.; from the East, 25; in the movies, 4, 5; the modern, 59f.; the Montana, 35; the myth of, 68–82; on the frontier, 140–41; the Texas, 11f., 35, 61, 74f., 76f., 91; use of fist, knife, gun, 97
Cowboy, etymology of the word: 73f.
Cowboy and His Interpreters, The (E. Douglas Branch): *viii*
Cowtowns: 47, 49, 76
Culley, John: 195
Cullum, Ridgewell: 176
Curly: A Story of the Arizona Desert (Roger Pocock): 62
Custer, General: 139; defeat by Sioux, 138–39

Dakota Territory: 49; Deadwood, 72, 125, 129–30; opening of Black Hills in, 139
Dale, Edward Everett: 70, 191–92
DeVoto, Bernard: 9, 164–65, 182–83
Debo, Angie: 191

Dime novel's use of Kit Carson, Calamity Jane, Deadwood
    Dick: 145
Dobie, J. Frank: *vii* f., 21–22, 161–62, 165, 175, 178–81, 182,
    188, 190, 196
Downs, Billy and California Ed, hanging of: 117

Earp, Wyatt: 126
Emmett, Chris: 192–93
Englishmen on the range: 62

Far West, the: 15
Fishwick, Marshall: 73, 183
Foote, Mary Hallock: 143
Fort Richardson, Texas: 136
Fort Sill, Oklahoma: 136
Freighting: 7, 127, 131–33; description of, 131; by Mormons,
    131; by Russell, Majors, and Waddell, 131
French, Warren: 147

Gabriel, Pete: 87f.
Gard, Wayne: *viii*, 191
Garland, Hamlin: 9, 169–71
Garrett, Pat: 95
Gates, Eleanor: 176
Geronimo: 52; and Apaches, 126; capture of, 137
Gipson, Fred: 59, 193
Goodnight, Charles: 38, 43, 51, 55, 68, 163, 198; wife of, 63
Graham-Tewkbury feud, basis of Zane Grey's *To the Last Man*
    and Dane Coolidge's *The Men Killers:* 113–14
Grangers: 107
Great American Desert: 10, 13, 16, 17, 18, 35
Great River (Paul Horgan): *viii*
Greeley, Horace: 18
Grey, Zane: 5, 9, 142, 171–74, 185
Grinnell, George Bird: 176
Gun fights: 77f., 87f.

Haley, J. Evetts: *viii*, 179, 189–90, 198n
Hardin, Wesley: 72
Harris, Frank: 179

Hastings, Frank: 195
Hickok, James B. (Wild Bill): 72, 85, 89ff., 125
Holladay, Ben: 130–31
Holliday, Doc: 126
Hollywood, California: 3–5
Horgan, Paul: *viii*, 23, 181f.
Horses: wrangling of, 37f.; Spanish mustangs, 11, 22f.
Hough, Emerson: 9, 26, 152–57; *North of 36*, 34, 53, 177, 181

Ibarra, Francisco de: 20
Iliff, John W.: 51, 68
Indians: 13, 16, 24, 42, 62, 85; country of, 30f., 138; dependence on buffalo, 133–34; frontier of, 133–37; movie versions of, 138
Indian tribes: Apache, 7, 16, 28, 52, 69, 135, 137; Mescalero Apache, 136; Arapahoe, 135; Cheyenne, 16, 135; Comanche, 7, 16, 34, 69, 135–36; Kiowa, 135–36; Lipan, 135; Sioux, 16, 69, 135, 138–39
Ingraham, Prentiss: 146f.

Jennings, Al J.: 176f.
Johannsen, Albert: 146

Kansas: 7, 10, 31, 39, 43, 44, 46, 49, 50, 71, 76–77, 88f.; Abilene, 6, 11, 31f., 46f., 72, 75, 89ff., 135; Baxter Springs, 29; Dodge City, 36, 42, 46f., 75, 77, 92ff., 126, 162–63; Ellsworth, 75, 92, 126; Hays City, 92; Newton, 75, 92; Wichita, 75, 126
Kansas City, Missouri: 27, 89

Lea, Tom: 177
Lewis, Alfred Henry: 9, 150–52, 170
Lighton, William R.: 176
"Little Joe the Wrangler": 7, 37
Lomax, John A.: 6
Longhorn cattle: 19ff., 23, 27, 39, 52, 113
Lorimer, George Horace: 168–69
Lynching: 116–20

Major, Mabel: 182
Majors, Alexander: 122, 131
Masterson, Bat: 126

Paterson, Arthur: 152
Patten, William G.: 147
Pattullo, George: 168–69, 182
Peake, Ora Brooks: 191
Pearce, T. M.: 182
Pelzer, Louis: 191
Peregrinaciones: 38
Phillips, Henry Wallace: 9, 164, 165–66
Phy, Joe: 87f.
Pike, Zebulon Montgomery: 18, 123
Pilgraim, Thomas (Arthur Morecamp): *Live Boys,* 144
"Pinto Trace" (Charles W. Webber): 85
Plains: Great Plains, 13, 16, 24, 48, 49, 50, 53, 54, 67, 78, 84, 88;
     Colorado Plains, 49; High Plains, 13, 16, 22, 46, 51; Lara-
     mie Plains, 52; Montana Plains, 49; the northern plains, 50,
     51, 62; settlement of the plains, 54f.; Staked Plains, 43;
     Wyoming Plains, 49
Pocock, Roger: 62, 176
Porter, William Sidney (O. Henry): 9, 167–68, 171

Queretaro: 38

Railroads: arrival of in West, 130; replace stagecoach, 130; re-
     frigerator car, 127; Atchison, Topeka, and Santa Fe, 92;
     Central Pacific, 130; Hannibal and St. Joseph, 31; Kansas
     Pacific, 31; Missouri Pacific, 30; Northern Pacific, 17; Un-
     ion Pacific, 49, 50, 51, 52, 72, 130
Raine, William McLeod: 171, 175
Ranches: A-K-X, 45; JA, 55, 61; King, 61; Matador, 61; New
     Mexico, 69; Spur, 63; Texas, 68; Three D, 61; XIT, 61, 104;
     dude, 5; life on, 48–67; housing of, 55; fence rider of, 56,
     59; fencing of, 55f., 115–16; in fiction, 142–43
Range, the: 48–67; cooking on, 37, 41; medical care on, 63; end
     of (open), 67; cattle industry on (between 1879 and
     1885), 105ff.
Rascoe, Burton: 185
Red Cloud (Sioux): 139
Remuda: 37f., 45
Rhodes, Eugene Manlove: 9, 142, 164–65, 175, 181, 183
Richter, Conrad: 177

Ridings, Sam P.: 191
Rivers: Arkansas, 42, 44; Brazos, 44; Canadian, 7, 44; Cimarron, 44; Colorado, 44; Concho, 43; Neches, 21, 28; North Canadian, 44; North Platte, 38, 44; Nueces, 18, 20; Pecos, 43, 44; Platte, 136; Red, 13, 21, 29, 32, 44, 46, 136; Rio Grande, 11, 13, 18, 20, 21, 74, 136; South Concho, 43; Stinkingwater, 44; Yellowstone, 13, 36
Rocky Mountains: 13f., 16, 49f.
Rodeos: 5
Rollins, Philip Ashton: 85
Roosevelt, Theodore: 5, 8, 25f., 76, 119, 124
Roundup: 56ff.
Russell, Charles M.: 197
Russell, William: 121
Russell, Majors, and Waddell: 16, 51, 131

Santa Fe Trail: 123, 131
Satanta, Satank, and Big Tree: capture of, 136
Saunders, George W.: 76
Scarborough, Dorothy: 177
Schaefer, Jack: 177
Seltzer, Charles Alden: 175
Sheepmen: treatment of by cattlemen, 111–15
Sherman, General William Tecumseh: 136
Shrine of Guadalupe: 38
Sibert, Bruce: 197
Sierra Nevada: 14, 50
Sinclair, Bertha Muzzy (B. M. Bower): 174–75
Siringo, Charles A.: 8, 196
Skinners: 73
Small, Joe: 194
Smith, Erwin: 168
Smith, Rebecca: 182
Smith, Thomas J.: 89f.
Sonnichsen, C. L.: 192
Spears, Frank Hamilton: 174
St. Louis, Missouri: 10, 27, 30, 31, 89
Stagecoaching: 127–30
Steinbeck, John: 177
Sterling, John: 92

Stuart, Granville: 35, 38, 79, 110, 117, 125, 195–96
Sugg, W. W.: 31

Texas: 11, 16, 18ff., 24, 26ff., 32f., 35, 39, 41, 43, 46ff., 57, 61, 66, 74, 76, 84f.; end of Indian threat in, 136–37; heart of ranch country in, 103–104; use of by Beadle and Adams, 147–48; Amarillo, 63; Brownsville, 18, 19; Corpus Christi, 19; Laredo, 18; San Antonio, 10, 18f., 46
Texas Panhandle: 38, 43
Texas Ranger: 94, 135
Thompson, Ben: 72, 90f., 92
Trail drives: 48; herding, 27f., 29, 33–47
Trail riders: 35–42
Treaty of Medicine Lodge: 135
True West (magazine): 194
Tucker, Patrick T.: 197
Tucker, Tommy: 36
Turner, Frederick Jackson: 12, 13, 14

United States mail service (pre-railroad): 127–28

Vigilantes: 116–20
Villalobos, Gregorio de: 20

Wallace, Governor Lew (of New Mexico): 95
Watson, Ella "Cattle Kate," and Jim Averill: hanging of, 118
Webb, Walter Prescott: 5, 10, 48, 80, 83, 162, 181–82, 186, 188
Webber, Charles W.: 85; *Tales of the Southern Border*, 143
Wellman, Paul: 136
Wells Fargo: 130
Western frontier: in relation to other frontiers, 123
Western movies: 5; stars of, Hopalong Cassidy, 3f.; Bill Hart, 71; Tex Ritter, 71; Tom Mix, 71; Roy Rogers, 4; Gene Autry, 4; Red Ryder, 4; The Lone Ranger, 4; *Red River*, 102
Western music: 5
Wheeler, Edward L.: 146
Whipple, T. K.: 173, 185, 186
White, Stewart Edward: 65, 166–67
Whittaker, Captain Frederick: 147